PROBLEMS OF AGING
Sociological and Social
Psychological Perspectives

PROBLEMS OF AGING
Sociological and Social Psychological Perspectives

1368

HERMAN J. LOETHER

California State College at Los Angeles

Dickenson Publishing Company, Inc., Belmont, California

27946

To my grandparents, Charles and Julia Loether,
eighty-seven years young

COVER BY WILLI BAUM

L.C. Cat. Card No.: 67–14174
Printed in the United States of America

Foreword

THIS series is based on the assumption that every instructor has his own ideas about the particular social problems that should receive treatment in a course on the subject. Any conventional text—and there are a number worthy of respect—prepackages the subject matter, so to speak. The instructor must either deal exclusively with those problems covered or skip some and introduce others through additional assigned readings. With this series, the instructor packages a social problems text to suit his needs. He selects those volumes which, in his judgment, should make up the course content. Each book covers one problem and stands by itself, dependent upon no cumulative carryover from any preceding volume.

There are several additional advantages in using a series of volumes rather than a single social problems text. In a series, a number of sociologists make separate contributions. Each is a specialist in his assigned subject. He can cover it in greater depth than would be possible were he limited to a single chapter of a conventional text. And since a variety of authors are represented, the student is exposed to different orientations. At the same time, each volume shares a common conceptual framework.

Van Nuys, California   David Dressler

Contents

Preface

Though problems of aging have always been with us, only during the past two decades has public awareness of these problems been heightened. Once problems become the concern of the public, they become social problems; and so it has been with problems of aging. As a result of this recent concern, a whole new field of scientific interest—the field of social gerontology—has evolved. The decades of the fifties and sixties have witnessed an outpouring of articles, books, monographs, readers, symposia, and conferences dealing with problems of aging. The heightened interest in and volume of research on aging almost demand that the subject be given attention in sociology courses. As a matter of fact, many sociology departments are introducing courses dealing specifically with social gerontology. This volume can serve as a useful source book for undergraduate courses in social problems. It should also be useful as supplementary reading for courses in social gerontology.

In a more specific sense, the book was written to fill the need for a survey of problems of aging from both the sociological and the social psychological perspectives. In spite of the great volume of published material available, there is no other single source that parallels this book in coverage and emphasis. Obviously, a book of this length cannot cover the subject in great depth. I have attempted to point out the major problems of aging and to explore the most relevant facets of these problems. I have not attempted to offer solutions to the problems, though at times I have suggested directions in which the solutions might lie. It is hoped that the material covered here will stimulate the reader's interest in the subject and motivate him to explore related sources for information.

The many published and unpublished works that have been of use to me in writing this book have been acknowledged in footnotes. In addition, there are several individuals who deserve special mention for the assistance they have given me in this endeavor.

I wish to thank Captain J. A. McAllister, Lieutenant G. G. Greeley, Sergeant J. P. Lovretovich, and Sergeant R. D. Mercer of the Los Angeles Police Department for supplying me with a wealth of information regarding schemes used to exploit the elderly.

Mrs. Alison K. Mauer of the Welfare Planning Council of Los Angeles gave generously of her time to share her expert knowledge of the housing problems of the elderly with me.

Ralph Thomlinson, David Dressler, and Mary Ellison read the manuscript and made suggestions that led to its improvement. Mrs. Ellison's "fly specking," in particular, did wonders for my syntax.

Finally, I must acknowledge my wife, Louise, and my son, Chris, for their encouragement and help. My wife was both my severest critic and my devoted typist. My son served me well as my most enthusiastic rooter.

If any flaws remain in this work, they are the fault of no one but myself.

H. J. L.

Chapter 1. The aging process

AGING is an inevitable and irreversible process. Since the fountain of youth continues to elude man, we must all be concerned with the prospect of growing old. Aging is not an event that takes place overnight, but a process that begins at the time of conception and continues throughout life.

In the early years of life and throughout young adulthood, we tend to view aging impersonally. It is something that happens to others, not to us. It is not until overt signs of aging, such as graying hair and bulging waistlines, make their appearance that we come to realize that it not only can, but *is* happening to us.

In the more traditional societies increasing age is accompanied by increasing prestige. In traditional Chinese society, the oldest members of the family were treated with reverence and respect. Much prestige was afforded the person who qualified to be called "old man."[1]

This is not the case in American society. Ours is a youth-oriented, work-oriented society. We revere those of strong body and sound health. Jack Benny's idea of the perennial thirty-ninth birthday is very popular. There is the general feeling that the older person is beyond that stage in life when he is best able to contribute to society; he is "over the hill."

Paradoxically, we prefer our political leaders to be older—but not too old. Many people thought that John F. Kennedy, at the age of 42, was too young to be president. However, only three times in our history have we elected a man as old as 65. William Henry Harrison was elected at the age of 67 (he died after serving one month of his term), and James Buchanan was elected at the age of 65. Dwight Eisenhower was 66 when he was elected to his second term in 1956. We apparently prefer men old enough to have the wisdom that usually comes with experience, but not so old that their vitality is on the wane.

It is interesting to note that, though Kennedy was thought to be too young to be president, he would have been too old for numerous other jobs. As a matter of fact, if he had been a professional athlete, at 42 he would have been considered "ancient."

As an outgrowth of our distaste for the idea of growing old we are

---

[1] Ernest W. Burgess and Harvey Locke, *The Family* (New York: The American Book Company, Inc., 1945), p. 44.

constantly in search of euphemisms for *old age*. Those who have worked with old people have found that they dare not call them old or elderly. We do not have *old people's clubs*, but *senior citizen's clubs*. We do not have *old* or *elderly* Americans, but *aging* Americans. No matter what words we use, however, we cannot escape the fact that we all grow old.

It is difficult to say at what point in life a person is old. Age is a biological, psychological, and sociological matter. Scientists have established that there are certain measurable biological changes that occur to the body as one ages. These changes include:

1. An increase in connective tissue in the organism.
2. A gradual loss of elastic properties of connective tissue.
3. A disappearance of cellular elements in the nervous system.
4. A reduction of the number of normally functioning cells.
5. An increased amount of fat.
6. A decrease in oxygen utilization.
7. A decrease in the amount of blood pumped, by the heart, under resting conditions.
8. A lesser amount of air expired by the lungs than in a younger organism.
9. A decreased muscular strength.
10. The excretion of hormones, especially by sex glands and the adrenal glands is lower than normal.[2]

These changes begin to occur in people at different chronological ages and progress at different rates. Some persons manifest some of these biological changes while they are still in their twenties; others do not begin to manifest them until much later.

Biological changes are only part of the story of aging. Psychological aspects of aging are important, too. There is probably some truth to the old adage, "You are only as old as you feel." At any rate, one's self-concept is an extremely important consideration in any discussion of aging. Is there any basis for including the woman who sees herself as "youngish" in the elderly category because she is 60 years of age? In many respects a person's self-concept is a more important index of his behavior than his chronological age or the biological changes that have taken place in his body. And it is the behavior associated with different age categories that makes age a significant concept.

Aging also has its sociological aspects. Age is a relative concept: to the teen-ager, the 30-year-old seems ancient, but the 30-year-old takes pleasure in the fact that he is still eligible for membership in the Young Democrats

[2] Kurt Wolff, *The Biological, Sociological and Psychological Aspects of Aging* (Springfield, Ill.: Charles C Thomas, 1959), p. 7.

or the Young Republicans. It was surely a 40-year-old who declared that "life begins at forty." Each age group looks at those age groups ahead of it as the *older generation*. This works until you get to the point where there is no age group ahead of you; then, you will probably have to admit that yours is the older generation—but not necessarily. There are people capable of deluding themselves even at that stage of life.

The important point is that age is a complicated concept with biological, psychological, and sociological connotations. Since aging is a process rather than an event, it is not possible to set a point in life when it can be said, "Starting today, you are old." By convention, the age of 65 is defined as that point in life. The age of 65, however, is at best a very rough index of old age.

Aging as a problem

Why has aging become a social problem? A social problem exists when the public recognizes it as such. Aging has been recognized as a social problem primarily because people are living longer now than they did in earlier times. The life expectancy for white males born in 1900 was 48 years; for white females, 51 years; for Negro males, 33 years; and for Negro females, 35 years. The corresponding life expectancies for those born in 1959 were 67 years for white males, 74 years for white females, 61 years for Negro males, and 66 years for Negro females. This means that the average life expectancy for Americans increased 21 years between 1900 and 1960.[3]

In 1900, the United States had about 3 million people (4.1 per cent of the population) who were 65 years of age or older. According to estimates made by the U.S. Bureau of the Census, the over-65 population reached 18 million (9.3 per cent) on January 1, 1965.[4] Next to children between the ages of 5 and 14, persons over 65 had the fastest rate of increase of any age category: their net increase was nearly 1,000 persons per day.[5]

At the turn of the century, the aged did not constitute a social problem because there were relatively few people who lived to the age of 65. The men who reached the age of 60 in 1900 could expect less than three years

[3] U.S. Bureau of the Census, *Statistical Abstract of the United States: 1961* (82d ed.; Washington, D.C., 1961), p. 56.
[4] Special Committee on Aging, United States Senate, *Developments in Aging: 1963 and 1964*, Senate Report No. 124 (Washington, D.C.: U.S. Government Printing Office, 1965), p. 1.
[5] Special Committee on Aging, United States Senate, *Developments in Aging: 1959 to 1963*, Senate Report No. 8 (Washington, D.C.: U.S. Government Printing Office, 1963), p. ix.

of life in retirement, in contrast to the eight years for men who reached 60 in 1960.[6] In 1900, men usually died before they reached the age of retirement. Retirement was so rare it had not yet become institutionalized. When it did occur, it was limited to those in the higher income brackets. It was probably the Social Security Act of 1935 that established 65 as the age of retirement.

The dramatic increase in life expectancy since 1900 can be attributed, in large part, to advances in medical science, sanitation, and nutrition. Great progress has been made in controlling, and in some cases, almost eliminating diseases that once snuffed out life at relatively early ages. As Thomlinson says,

The leading causes of death have not always been the same. . . . Famine, typhus, smallpox, and the plague—now virtually controllable—once ravaged mankind. Other scourges have also been conquered or are on their way out, for example, typhoid, tuberculosis, cholera, dysentery, influenza, and pneumonia. . . . The respiratory diseases (influenza, pneumonia, and tuberculosis) have lost their dominance, dropping from the top of the list to relatively obscure ranks. Circulatory ailments and cancer now are responsible together for more than half of all deaths in the United States.[7]

Science has made the greatest strides in controlling those diseases that attack persons of *all* ages. The diseases that remained among the top killers in 1960 were those that take their greatest toll among older people. In 1960, one's chances of surviving to a more advanced age were greater, and so, too, were one's chances of contracting a circulatory disease or cancer.

Although, percentage-wise, persons over 65 are still a definite minority, there are enough of them, in terms of absolute numbers, to make their presence felt. It is their current and potential influence that has aroused the awareness of the American people to the social problems of old age.

Recognition of and concern for the problems faced by old people led Congress to pass the Older Americans Act of 1965. This act provided for the establishment of an Administration on Aging within the Department of Health, Education, and Welfare. The act declared as objectives for older Americans: (1) "an adequate income," (2) "the best possible physical and mental health," (3) "suitable housing," (4) "full restorative

[6] Special Staff on Aging, U.S. Department of Health, Education, and Welfare, *The Nation and Its Older People: Report of the White House Conference on Aging,* January 9–12, 1961 (Washington, D.C.: U.S. Government Printing Office, 1961), p. 117.

[7] Ralph Thomlinson, *Population Dynamics: Causes and Consequences of World Demographic Change* (New York: Random House, Inc., 1965), pp. 106–107.

(rehabilitative) services" (5) "opportunity for employment without age discrimination," and (6) "retirement in health, honor and dignity."[8]

Two perspectives on the problem

Aging can be viewed as a social problem from two perspectives. First, aging is a direct problem to that segment of the population which is in the aged category. Of course, this aspect of the problem should be of concern to everyone, because every person who survives long enough will become a member of the aged segment of the population.

Second, aging is a social problem for society as a whole, because the presence of old people and their problems has profound effects upon the structure and functioning of society.

Advancing age is accompanied by changing circumstances and their attendant problems. Profound changes take place in a person's interpersonal relations as he grows older. His relations with the members of his family change. His parents die. His children reach adulthood and strike out on their own. Upon the birth of grandchildren, he assumes the status of grandparent. At some point, the older person is faced with the loss of the spouse. Friendships change as the years pass. Contact is lost with some friends; others die. Retirement leads to the severance of ties with work associates. Patterns of community participation change.

Health problems become more frequent and acute with the passing years. The physical and mental processes deteriorate. Increases in expenditures for medical care and medicines become necessary at that time in life when income is likely to be most limited.

Living arrangements frequently change as one grows older. Some older persons who have their own homes are able to maintain them. Many, however, through choice or necessity, move in with relatives, to retirement communities, to apartments, to rooming houses, or to homes for the aged. Changes in living accommodations often give rise to personal and social problems.

Employment is a serious problem facing older people. Changing technology and labor-market demands may leave the older worker in a state of vocational obsolescence. Automation is a case in point. Many older workers are being automated out of their jobs. The unemployed older worker is hard pressed to find another job. Today's expanding job opportunities are

[8] Julius Horwitz, "This is the Age of the Aged," *The New York Times Magazine*, May 16, 1965, pp. 82–86.

in specialties for which older persons are not trained. There is reluctance to retrain older workers for new jobs because of their limited work lives.

Related to the employment problem is the problem of retirement. Generally, retirement is a traumatic experience for one who has spent many years in the labor force; some persons look upon retirement as the prelude to death. Even those who look forward to retirement may find the adjustment process difficult.

Older persons are frequently the targets of exploiters and confidence men. Life savings are often swallowed up by get-rich-quick schemes, medical quacks, and pie-in-the-sky movements. Senescence, with its accompanying infirmity and frequent physical and social isolation, makes older people particularly vulnerable. Perhaps this is the reason for the old chestnut, "There's no fool like an old fool."

Eventually, old age brings everyone face to face with life's final tribulation—death. The elderly person is confronted by the deaths of his friends and loved ones as well as by his own inevitable demise.

One of the major purposes of this book is to look at problems such as these that face old people. We will seek to determine the sources of these problems and to analyze the effects they have on the lives of old people in Chapters 2 through 8.

The second aspect of the problem of aging is also extremely important, that is, the effects the presence of old people and their problems have on society as a whole. We are interested in the economic, political, and social influences our older citizens exert on our society at large. The interests, desires, and needs of the elderly tend to differ from those of other segments of the population. As the elderly increase in number, they exert proportionately greater pressure on society to meet their demands. This aspect of the problem of aging obviously deserves our attention. What difference does the existence of these problems confronting old people make to American society? What changes have resulted from the existence of old people and their problems? These are significant questions, and they need to be examined. It is not enough to examine problems of aging in the narrow context of their effects upon the aged. We must also look at these problems in a broader context. From time to time, throughout the book, we will examine the problems of aging in their broader context. However, the last chapter in particular will be concerned with the effects of our older citizens and their problems on the structure and functioning of American society.

Chapter 2. Interpersonal relations

SHAKESPEARE said:

> All the world's a stage,
> And all the men and women merely players:
> They have their exits and their entrances:
> And one man in his time plays many parts.[1]

In other words, we are the players in the ongoing drama called life. Each of the parts we play is a *social role*. A social role consists of the pattern of behavior expected of a person taking part in a social situation. For example, the position of president of the United States carries with it a set of duties, obligations, and rights. These duties, obligations, and rights constitute an expected behavior pattern for the person filling the position of president.

Each person plays many roles. Among them are sex roles, age roles, family roles, occupational roles, religious roles, and political roles. Some of these roles are widely shared, such as the male role, or the role of citizen of the United States. Other roles are shared by relatively few persons. For example, few persons have filled the role of president of the United States. Furthermore, this role cannot be played by more than one person at a time.

The sum total of a person's social roles will be referred to as his *role complex*. It is neither possible nor desirable for a person to play, simultaneously, all of the roles in his role complex. The individual plays those roles that are appropriate to the social situation in which he finds himself and holds the other roles in his role complex in abeyance.

Some roles are largely involuntary, that is, they are played continuously and cannot be easily avoided. Examples of such roles are those of sex and age. These roles are shared by large categories of persons and are not limited to particular social organizations. The involuntary nature of these roles is largely due to the fact that the individual's appearance offers visible evidence that they are part of his role complex. For example, the male is

---

[1] William Shakespeare, *As You Like It*, Act II, Scene VII.

not usually able to hide his gender; thus, he is expected to behave as a male. Within broad categories, a person's age may be estimated, and he is expected to "act his age."

Other roles are voluntary in that they can be played or not played according to the wishes of the individual. In this category fall social roles associated with particular social organizations. A person may or may not play his occupational role, as he wishes. The married man may play the husband role or not, as he wishes.

On occasion, a person may play two or more voluntary roles simultaneously, although generally such roles are played in turn. In the presence of his children a man will play the father role and in the presence of his wife, the husband role. However, if both wife and children are present, he may choose to play both husband and father roles simultaneously.

As a person moves through the various stages of the life cycle, his role complex changes. New roles are added and old ones discarded. The infant role gives way to the child's role, the child's role to the adolescent's role, and the adolescent's role to the adult's role. During the periods of childhood and adolescence and, possibly through young adulthood, the person will play the student role. Upon reaching maturity, most persons assume occupational roles. Family roles, likewise, change. The son eventually becomes a husband and father—and later, a grandfather. It is our peculiar complex of social roles which makes us an integral part of society. As our role complex changes, our relationship to our society also changes.

Our self-concept depends, in large part, upon which roles we play. Our sex role, age role, occupational role, family role, and others supply us with an identity. Our individual perceptions of this identity constitute our self-concept. Changes in our role complex lead to alterations in our self-concept.

Changes in an individual's role complex and the attendant changes in his self-concept may constitute a problem at any stage of the life cycle. However, such problems appear to be particularly frequent and acute among the aged. It is the purpose of this chapter (1) to examine the changes in the role complex which accompany increasing age, and (2) to study the problems arising out of such changes.

Changing family roles

There is an extremely important cluster of social roles which derive from our family relationships. Most people, at some time in their lives, play son or daughter roles, brother or sister roles, husband or wife roles, father or mother roles, and grandfather or grandmother roles. Such roles tend to be enduring but not unchanging. As we progress through the various stages of the life cycle, each of our family roles tends to change qualitatively. In the pages that follow we shall examine three of these family roles in particular —those of spouse, parent, and grandparent.

Most adults, sooner or later, assume the spouse role. The relations between spouses gradually change as a marriage lasts over the years. There is a qualitative difference in the relations between newlyweds and the relations between a couple married for some time. The first year of marriage apparently is the crucial one, because the peak period in divorce rates is reached in the second year of marriage. There is a dramatic decline in divorce rates after five years of marriage. During these early years, successful and enduring adaptations are made in the relations between spouses, or the marriage is dissolved.

The birth of children leads to further changes in the relations between spouses. Symptomatic of the change is the tendency for the spouses to call each other mother and dad or equivalent names. The presence of children leads to an additional source of common interest and concern. Occasionally, in fact, the motivation for having children is to relieve strained marital relations and to put the marriage on a sounder footing.

Children in the home lead to profound alterations in the uses of leisure time. Mobility tends to be decreased. The night life that is enjoyed by the childless couple becomes inconvenient and expensive for the couple with children. Baby-sitters bite into the funds available for leisure-time activities. There is a tendency to switch to the kinds of activities which can be engaged in by the family as a unit. For several years, while the children are young, it is necessary to plan family activities around them. The occasions where husband and wife can do things together without the children may be very few and, for that reason, may take on special significance.

As the children get older, the occasions when the husband and wife may do things together alone increase. The relations between spouses may again begin to take on some of the flavor of the relations between the childless couple. There is a definite freeing effect (although it may not be viewed as such) once the children marry and leave home.

One of the most significant changes that has taken place since the turn of the century has been the lengthening of the marriage relationship. Men and women marry earlier and stay married longer. The average gain in married life has been about 10 years.[2] The number of children in the family has decreased, and the last child marries sooner. In the average

---

[2] Meyer F. Nimkoff, "Changing Family Relationships of Older People in the United States during the Last Forty Years," in Clyde B. Vedder, ed., *Gerontology: A Book of Readings* (Springfield, Ill.: Charles C. Thomas, 1963), p. 112.

family of 1890, the last child married about two years after the death of one parent. In 1950, the last child married between 13 and 14 years before the death of either parent.[3] This means that in 1890 the average husband and wife had no time together after their children married and left home, while in 1950 the average couple had 13 or 14 years together after the last child left home. Furthermore, in 1950 there was less of a tendency for married children to live with their parents than at the turn of the century.

This period after the last child has left home is often seized upon as the opportunity to do "all the things we had planned to do, but couldn't because of the children."

A new dimension develops in the relations between husband and wife when the husband retires. Prior to retirement, the husband generally spends his days away from home, and home is the domain of the wife. The wife experiences some change in her household routine when the last of her children leaves home; but her cleaning and cooking continue on an altered scale.

The wife is faced with a new and unique situation after the retirement of her husband in that, for the first time in their married life, he is home during the day. For the first time he may intrude upon her daily routine. Problems frequently arise with respect to the roles to be played by the husband and wife in maintaining the home. For some women, the presence of the husband offers the opportunity to share some of the household drudgery. For others, his presence might be looked upon as an invasion of woman's proper domain. Some husbands adjust to the situation by developing daily routines outside the home, to stay out of the wife's way and allow her routine to continue substantially unchanged. Others stay at home and seek to carve out a section of the domain which they may call their own.

Some marriages survive over the years largely because there is a regular daily separation of the worlds of the husband and wife. The spouses are able to make a tolerable adjustment to each other because they do not see too much of each other. The husband may look forward to work as an opportunity to get away from his wife for a while, and the wife may send the husband on his way with a sigh of relief to have him out of the way for the day. For such marriages, retirement can constitute a very real crisis. The years of retirement may be spent together in an armed truce, in a pattern of studied avoidance, or in extreme cases, the marriage may end in a belated divorce.

Assuming that adequate funds are available, the retired couple may

[3] *Ibid.*

partake of extended travel to "do things we have always wanted to do and see places we have always wanted to see." For most retired couples, however, limited financial resources rule out the possibility of carrying out long-dreamed-of activities. Thus, the burden of adjustment is placed upon the husband-wife relationship itself.

When it is not possible to submerge problems of interpersonal relations in a whirlwind of activity, the relations between husband and wife must be faced head on and some satisfactory adaptation must be made.

Another important family role, that of parent, is added to the role complex when the first child is born. Striking qualitative changes take place in the parental role, too, as the person progresses through the various stages of the life cycle. Husbands and wives who exhibit carefree and irresponsible behavior patterns before parenthood may show definite signs of "settling down" after the birth of a child. For most persons, parenthood is a sobering responsibility. Few can help but be impressed by the thought that a helpless infant is dependent upon them.

As the years pass and the children get older, their dependence upon the parent decreases. Their increasing independence is often more apparent to the children than it is to the parents. In the early days of life, children's interpersonal relations are limited, largely, to members of the immediate family. When the children reach school age, however, their interpersonal relations begin to take on broader dimensions. The school, in effect, helps children to branch out and assert their independence. An important function of our formal educational system is to prepare young people to "cut the apron strings" and launch out on their own. Education gradually dissolves the myth of parental omniscience and omnipotence. Mother and Dad are put in their proper perspective as ordinary mortals.

"Cutting the apron strings" is often more difficult for the parents than it is for the children. The child's social world is gradually expanding, and his parents come to occupy an increasingly less important part in it. The social world of the parents is relatively less expansive. It may have already reached its broadest dimensions at the time the first child was born and may have contracted somewhat as the parents focused their attention on their offspring. In the last analysis, the parents may have become more dependent upon their children than the children upon their parents.

It is more frequently the mother than the father who has difficulty adjusting to the fact that her babies are babies no longer. Most men structure their lives around their jobs and therefore have difficulty adjusting to retirement. Women, on the other hand, frequently structure their lives around their children, and it is the loss of the active mother role that is traumatic to them.

When the child marries, his primary identification shifts from his family of orientation to his family of procreation. His concern for his parents becomes secondary to his concern for his own wife and children. His own family responsibilities may conflict with obligations felt toward his parents. In this case, he may be forced to neglect such obligations. It may be difficult for Mother and Dad to accept the fact that the married child has assumed family responsibilities that take precedence over his obligations toward them. The reluctance of the child to come running when Mother calls may be interpreted as ingratitude. An innocent daughter-in-law may be accused of alienating the son's affections for his parents.

A related problem is the role conflict to which the married child, the male in particular, is subjected when he finds himself in the presence of mother and wife at the same time. Mother still looks upon him as her little boy and expects him to behave accordingly, but his wife expects him to behave as a self-sufficient man. If he elects to play the little-boy role for Mother, he strains his relations with his wife. If he elects to play the husband role, his mother may interpret his behavior as a rejection of her.

It takes a perceptive and mature parent to adapt successfully to the qualitative changes in the parent role which accompany the loss of children through marriage. Many parents (particularly mothers) are not capable of such adaptations. Is it any wonder that the mother-in-law problem has become a great American institution?

Many mothers adapt to the loss of the active mother role through the substitution of other roles. For some, the departure of the last child from the home is followed by a plunge into social, religious, or philanthropic activities. For others, it marks a return to, or an initial entry, into the labor force. Gertrude Bancroft found that "women with no children under 18 years at home, including both the recently married and those whose children had grown up, were, of course, most likely to be regular full-time workers (43.9 per cent in 1955)."[4]

Some indication that these women are not working strictly because of financial need is given by the fact that their presence in the labor force is not directly dependent upon the husband's income. Bancroft comments, "Available data suggest that a married woman's decision to enter the labor force is influenced more by whether or not she has young children than it is by the amount of her husband's income or by his occupation."[5]

Another interesting phenomenon that might be related to the parents' need to compensate for the departure of children from the home is the tendency for some older couples to shower their attentions upon pets. Persons who seem indifferent toward pets during their younger years often

[4] *The American Labor Force: Its Growth and Changing Composition* (New York: John Wiley & Sons, Inc., 1958), p. 126.
[5] *Ibid.*, p. 124.

develop a sharply increased interest in them after the children leave home. Many badly pampered dogs owe their enviable circumstances, indirectly at least, to the emancipation of the last child.

Another role the aging may use to compensate for the loss of the active parent role is that of the grandparent. For many, the grandparent role is more pleasurable than the parent role. It is looked upon as an opportunity to enjoy one's relations with children without having to assume responsibility for them. As many a grandparent has said, "I have done my job of raising my own children, now I am going to *enjoy* my grandchildren."

In addition to the relaxation of responsibility which accompanies the grandparent role, there is a certain amount of prestige that attaches to it. The grandparent role, among peers, has about it an aura of maturity and stability. The person who has become a grandparent may take great pleasure in flaunting his new status before the members of his peer group who have not yet become grandparents. And of course, there are those inevitable pictures of the grandchildren to which friends and strangers alike are subjected.

Like parenthood, grandparenthood often leads to profound changes in behavior and accompanying alterations in the self-concept. The new grandmother who, in the past, meticulously rinsed her hair to conceal graying and assiduously tended to her waistline, may now let her hair turn gray to give her "that distinguished look" and give her waistline free rein. The stern, unbending father may, miraculously, become the doting and permissive grandfather. Behavior considered intolerable in children may be viewed with amusement in grandchildren. There may be definite signs that the old man has mellowed.

As Nimkoff has pointed out, there has been a qualitative change in the grandparent-grandchild relationship since 1900.[6] Because the birth and death rates have been lowered, the grandparents of today have fewer grandchildren than those of 1900 and the grandchildren of today are more likely to have living grandparents. Not only is the grandparent-grandchild relationship of today of longer duration, but the grandparent has fewer grandchildren upon whom to bestow his attentions. There is potential, at least, for a closer relationship between grandparent and grandchild because the child of today has less competition. Paradoxically, however, the greater rate of social change now, compared to the turn of the century, has led to a greater communication gap between persons of different generations. Then too, grandparent and grandchild are less likely to live in close proximity.

Children who look upon their parents as members of the older generation may consider grandparents to be relics of the prehistoric past. The fact

[6] *Op. cit.*, p. 117.

that our society is oriented toward youth and the future has aggravated problems of grandparent-grandchild interpersonal relations. The problem, however, is not one of an antagonistic relationship between grandchild and grandparent. It is, rather, a problem of the grandparent's being considered a curiosity out of the past or—worse yet—being ignored.

The change in the structure of the American family from the extended- to the nuclear-family pattern has produced a relatively greater change in the grandfather role than in the grandmother role. In the extended family system, the grandfather is frequently the head of the household. His is a patriarchal position, which commands respect and obedience from other members of the family. Although this extended family system still exists in other societies, it has, for all practical purposes, disappeared from the American scene. The common pattern in this country is now the nuclear family, limited to two generations: parents and children. It is the father (or the mother) who now fills the position of head of the household. Grandfather may still be the head of his own household, but he has little or no control over his married children. Even when he lives with married children, he is relegated to a subsidiary role in the family.

This situation has led to a virtual disappearance of the sharp distinction that once existed between the grandfather and grandmother roles. The grandfather role has been reduced from one of authority to one in which he is playmate and baby-sitter for his grandchildren. Since grandmother can also play the role of baby-sitter and playmate, there is little substantive difference between the grandmother and the grandfather roles. The lack of a uniquely masculine flavor to the grandfather role may be an added impediment to successful adjustment among the aged.

Changing community roles

Aging results in changes not only in one's family roles but in one's whole role complex. People prefer to associate with others like themselves. Interpersonal relations tend to develop among persons who share common attitudes and interests. Also, persons who play similar roles tend to develop friendships. Neighbors who are parents of small children may develop friendships largely because they share similar parental roles. Married couples tend to socialize with other married couples. Couples with grown children tend to socialize with other couples with grown children.

One of the most significant events in the life of the aging man is retirement. Major changes in interpersonal relations occur as a result of retirement. For many men their most important interpersonal relations, outside their family relations, arise directly from their work situations. Satisfaction with one's work may result from satisfying interpersonal relations with fellow workers rather than from the job itself. To a man who values the comradeship of his fellow workers, retirement can be a traumatic experience.

Though he may vow to maintain contact with his former work associates, the retired man probably will not do so. Retirement means more than physical separation from fellow workers; it also means a qualitative change in social relationships. Should he return to the work situation to visit his former comrades, he is likely to find that he does not fit into the group any more. The work role is a necessary prerequisite to participation in the interpersonal relations of the work group. One who no longer plays the work role, regardless of former status, is an outsider.

Interpersonal relations developed on the job may extend beyond the work situation. Fellow workers and their spouses may visit each other's homes and participate in recreational activities together. These relations are more likely to endure beyond retirement than those which are limited to the job situation. However, these relations may also fade eventually. If the job is the central motivation for shared activities outside the work situation, the workers may find that they no longer have much in common after one or both of them has retired. The bond that made visiting together pleasant might have been shop talk. If one of the men is now retired, he may enjoy talking to the other about current happenings on the job. After a while, however, he may find that he is not familiar with those now on the job and may have increasing difficulty keeping up his end of the conversation. If both men are retired, they may reminisce about how things were on the job. But, after a while, they may find that their reminiscences no longer give them much satisfaction. Once their common job experiences fade into insignificance, their friendship may follow suit. In situations like this, the woman also loses something in interpersonal relations. Friendships she has formed with wives of her husband's fellow workers are likely to fade once her husband retires. It is the man, however, who is generally harder hit by the social consequences of retirement.

Zena Smith Blau, in a study of 468 men and women aged 60 and over from Elmira, New York, found that retirement led to an alteration in self-concept.[7] Blau asked her subjects whether the people who were important to them thought of them as being old and whether the subjects thought of themselves as being old. She found that those who considered themselves old believed that significant others also considered them old. Moreover, retired persons were more likely to consider themselves old than those who

[7] "Changes in Status and Age Identification," *American Sociological Review*, XXI (1956), pp. 198–203.

were still employed. Of the subjects under 70, more than one-third of the retired considered themselves old, in contrast to less than one-fifth of the employed. Of the subjects over 70, two-thirds of the retired considered themselves old, compared to two-fifths of the employed.[8]

Self-concept is a significant factor in the determination of a person's interpersonal relations. The person who considers himself middle-aged will associate with others whom he sees as being middle-aged. The person who considers himself old will associate with other "old" people. The change in self-concept accompanying retirement often isolates the retired person from others because of his tendency to see himself as old. This fact may explain the tendency for older men to be more isolated than older women. For women, the husband's retirement does not serve as a bench mark separating middle age and old age.

Since people tend to associate with others who play similar roles, marital status is an important determinant of interpersonal relations. Married couples tend to associate with married couples and to participate in those activities which require a partner. The immediate consequence is that the old maid or the old bachelor is not likely to be included in the interpersonal relations of the married. The older bachelor must rely for his interpersonal relations upon persons who share his marital status, or on members of his family. As he grows older, his bachelor friends grow fewer in number and his social isolation tends to increase. It is a generally accepted principle that the unmarried are more likely than the married to be socially isolated. Not only are they without a marriage partner; they also tend to have fewer friends. An additional finding of the Blau study was that older persons who did not belong to friendship groups were more likely to consider themselves old than those who did belong.[9] Since people who consider themselves old tend to interact with others less often than those who do not consider themselves old, a vicious spiral tends to operate. The person who does not have friends tends to see himself as old, and the person who sees himself as old is less likely to form friendships with others. Consequently, the already isolated person is faced with deepening social isolation.

A study by Marjorie Fiske Lowenthal of the Langley Porter Neuropsychiatric Institute may have important implications for the problem of social isolation. She found that having a confidant was more important for mental health, self-image, and morale than having much social interaction with others.[10] This finding would seem to indicate that the quality of an

---

[8] *Ibid.*, p. 200.

[9] *Ibid.*, p. 201.

[10] "Isolation and Adjustment in Old Age," paper presented at the annual meeting of the Western Gerontological Society, Los Angeles, Calif., November 13, 1965.

old person's interpersonal relations is more important than the quantity. One close friend upon whom one can rely can be more important than a large number of casual acquaintances.

Widowhood produces significant changes in one's interpersonal relations. The widowed person does not fit in socially with married couples, even those who were close friends before the death of the spouse. The activities in which married couples participate often require partners. For instance, square dancing is a popular form of recreation among older married couples. Unless widowed persons can find partners acceptable to married friends, they are likely to become increasingly isolated from those interpersonal relations in which they and their spouses participated.

Many more widows than widowers are confronted by problems of interpersonal relations. Whereas 12.7 per cent of men between 65 and 74 were widowers in 1960, 44.4 per cent of the women in the same category were widows.[11] As age increases, the discrepancy becomes more marked. The facts that men marry younger women and that the life expectancy for women is about five years longer than it is for men means that a woman is much more likely to spend her last years as a widow than a man as a widower.

Perhaps it is the fact that widows are so much more numerous than widowers among the aged that has led to the institutionalization of the widow's status in our society. Because most married women face the prospect of widowhood, they may be better prepared for it. At any rate, widows seem to make successful adjustments more often than widowers. As a rule, widows are more gregarious and more ready to participate in social activities than are widowers. The membership rolls of senior citizens' clubs are made up overwhelmingly of women. This is explainable, in part, because of the preponderance of women in the older age categories. But even beyond that, there seems to be less tendency for older men than women to participate. Perhaps the few men who do so are those who are still married and participate under pressure from their spouses.

The widower who is determined not to spend his last years in loneliness is in a good position to find himself another wife. In the age groups over 65 there are fewer than 90 men per 100 women in the population. This, added to the fact that men marry younger women, means that many unattached women are available for courting. The older woman's prospect of finding a new mate is somewhat gloomy, for she faces a great deal of competition in her search.

Remarriage is one solution to the problem of loneliness in old age. The facts indicate that it is a solution increasingly turned to. Such marriages are

[11] U.S. Bureau of the Census, *Statistical Abstract of the United States: 1961* (82d ed.; Washington, D.C., 1961), p. 34.

becoming more acceptable in our society. Perhaps the advent of retirement hotels and communities in which eligible persons are thrown into contact with each other has helped to accelerate this trend.

A debatable question facing the old person is whether he should seek friends among younger people or associate largely with people his own age. Some experts in gerontology take the position that the older person will feel more comfortable and will make a better adjustment to old age if he associates primarily with his peer group. They argue that old people and young people live in different worlds, enjoy different things, and are best off with their own kind. The underlying philosophy of the retirement community movement is that adjustment to old age is facilitated by living in communities limited to older persons.

The opposite position is that age is a state of mind, and that the older person who associates with younger people will retain the mental outlook of youth. There is fear that the old person surrounded by old people will define himself as old and begin to behave accordingly. One difficulty with this second approach is that if the older person is not accepted by younger people, the rebuff may have a deleterious effect upon his self-concept. He may begin to feel even older than he would ordinarily.

A third alternative is a more natural situation in which the older person has contact with both younger people and people his own age. In this situation he may be able to enjoy the company of persons of all ages without serious danger of being rebuffed for not acting his age. Without question this third situation is most natural. However, which of the three situations is most beneficial for the adjustment of older persons has yet to be determined. It is one of those important but unanswered questions of gerontology.

Two theories of adjustment to aging

Two current theories seek to describe the process through which people adjust to the fact of aging. Though they emphasize different aspects of the adjustment problem, these theories supplement each other. Both focus on the individual's role complex and on the changes that take place in it as the person ages. One theory is referred to as disengagement theory, the other as the theory of role flexibility.

In their book, *Growing Old*, Elaine Cumming and William Henry have outlined the *theory of disengagement*.[12] The gist of this theory is that as a

[12] (New York: Basic Books, Inc., 1961).

person ages, he begins to withdraw from society by surrendering some of his social roles. Cumming and Henry say that disengagement is an inevitable process, in which many of the relationships between a person and other members of society are severed and those which remain are altered in quality.[13] As a person gets older, he begins to face up to the inevitability of death and begins preparing for it by gradually withdrawing from active societal roles. Furthermore, the disengagement process is accelerated by declining health and motility.

Because of differences among individuals, the time in life at which the disengagement process begins and the rate at which it proceeds vary. Also, the degree of qualitative change which occurs in enduring interpersonal relations differs from person to person. Cumming and Henry state that, once it has begun, the disengagement process becomes self-perpetuating.

Since the occupational role is central for most men, while the family roles are central for most women, it is postulated that there will be significant differences in the disengagement processes of men and women.

In our society, success is judged on the basis of knowledge and skill. The individual plays an instrumental role in society as long as he has the necessary knowledge and skills to contribute. According to the theory, age is usually accompanied by declining knowledge and skill, so that there are societal pressures on the aging individual to disengage himself from his instrumental roles.

By the same token, as an individual ages, his self-concept is altered. When he comes to see himself as old, he is likely to perceive his knowledge and skill as declining and may begin the disengagement process on his own volition.

The disengagement process may be initiated by the individual, by the society, or both. If both the individual and society are ready for disengagement at the same time, the result is successful disengagement. If neither the individual nor society is ready, the individual remains engaged. There are two possibilities of disjunction between the expectations of the individual and those of society. The individual may be prepared to disengage before society expects him to, in which case engagement is likely to continue. However, society may expect the individual to disengage before he is ready. In this case, disengagement is the likely result. Cumming and Henry postulate that the first type of disjunction is more common among women while the second is more common among men.

If society disengages the individual from his central life role—work for men and family roles for women—before he is ready, he is likely to experience a significant decline in morale. However, he may still make a successful adjustment to his disengaged state if he is able to substitute

---

[13] *Ibid.*, p. 211.

suitable new roles for those he has lost. Finally, the more intricately the individual's self-concept and image of personal success are related to the roles from which he is disengaged, the more traumatic the disengagement process will be for him.

Robert J. Havighurst has focused on what he calls *role flexibility* as the key to successful adjustment to aging.[14] In research he conducted in conjunction with Ruth Albrecht, Havighurst found that those individuals who were active in a wide variety of social roles or who were highly active in a given social role were more likely to be happy and to make a good social adjustment to old age than those who were less active.[15]

He points out that significant changes occur in an individual's role complex between the ages of 50 and 75. Some roles are reduced or discontinued, some are intensified, others are intensified with effort, and still others are assumed for the first time. Some older persons intensify their homemaker roles (e.g., by gardening, decorating, repairing, or entertaining); others play more active roles in their churches. Roles that may be intensified with some effort include roles as citizens, members of friendship groups, and members of extended families. Participation in recreational activities may be increased. Creative activities may be undertaken. Among the roles likely to be reduced or discontinued are the roles of worker, parent, and spouse. Among the new roles that might be assumed for the first time are the grandparent role and the role of member of a senior citizen's organization. Havighurst says: "For most people, the set of habits which constitutes a role is changed only with difficulty. To change roles easily and increase or reduce activity in a given role requires a personal quality which we shall call 'role flexibility.' "[16]

How is this quality called role flexibility acquired? According to Havighurst, role flexibility can best be cultivated in the middle years through a reasonably successful variety of role-playing experiences. He cautions that too much success in playing a particular role may lead to rigidity rather than role flexibility. For instance, the highly successful business man may have difficulty adjusting to old age and retirement because his occupational role is too important a part of his life experience. A deliberate plan of action during the middle years in which a variety of new roles are explored and a variety of new interests are developed presumably will lead to role flexibility and help the individual to make a successful transition from middle age to old age.

[14] "Flexibility and the Social Roles of the Retired," *American Journal of Sociology*, LIX (1954), pp. 309–311.
[15] *Older People* (New York: Longmans, Green & Co., 1953), chaps. III, VI, and XVII.
[16] "Havighurst, *op. cit.*, p. 310.

Though they stress different aspects of the adjustment process, the disengagement theory and the theory of role flexibility are not incompatible; in fact, they supplement each other nicely. The disengagement theory describes the process by which the individual's role complex is voluntarily or involuntarily altered as he grows old. Cumming and Henry's description of the disjunctions that occur between the expectations of society and those of the individual accounts very neatly for the many cases of poor adjustment among aged individuals. Havighurst's theory of role flexibility, on the other hand, serves to explain why many persons who are involuntarily disengaged from their central life roles are still able to make successful adjustments to old age. According to Havighurst, these are the people who have cultivated that personal quality called role flexibility.

Chapter 3. Health

At first glance it might appear that health is strictly a physical or medical rather than a social problem. There are definite physical aspects to most health problems, but there are also important social and psychological aspects. From the social and psychological standpoints, the physical evidence of illness or disease may be largely irrelevant. In studying behavior, the person's beliefs about his health may be more significant than his actual health status as evaluated objectively.

The person suffering from a disease does not alter his self-concept or his behavior until he becomes aware of the disease. Many people who are victims of heart disease, for example, are unaware of their malady and go on living normal lives until there is some outward manifestation of their problem. Others who have no heart disease, but who think they have, make profound adjustments in both their self-concept and behavior.

Illness is institutionalized as a social role. Talcott Parsons describes the set of behavior expectations attaching to the "sick role." He lists four aspects of the "institutionalized expectation system relative to the sick role":[1] 1. There is the expectation that the sick individual will be unable to fulfill his normal social responsibilities, and furthermore, that he should not try to fulfill them. 2. It is assumed that the individual cannot make himself well by an act of will; his condition is such that he must be taken care of. 3. Being ill is undesirable, and the individual has an obligation to want to get well. 4. The sick individual has an obligation to seek competent medical help, usually from a physician. Moreover, he has an obligation to cooperate with the physician so that he will regain his health.

The significant social fact about health is that people who see themselves as being well will play the well role, and people who see themselves as being sick will play the sick role. Of course, a person's perception of the state of his health depends partly on how others perceive his health. An individual may begin to think of himself as being in poor health because others treat him as though he were in poor health. On the other hand, an individual whose health is objectively poor may see himself as being in good health because others treat him as though his health were good.

The person whose own evaluation of his health is incongruent with the

[1] *The Social System* (Glencoe, Ill.: The Free Press, 1951), p. 436.

evaluations of others will generally make some adaptation aimed at increasing congruency. He may change his own evaluation, he may convince others that they are wrong about his condition, he may seek out others who will agree with his evaluation, or he may discredit the opinions of others. The single most important evaluation affecting the person's own conception of his health is usually the evaluation made by a physician. In spite of the fact that one's friends and relatives may not see him as being sick, if he feels that he is sick and his physician agrees that he is sick, then he will probably be satisfied that he is, in fact, sick.

There is a fairly general belief in our society that illness is a part of being old. Old age is seen as the time in life when one's health progressively deteriorates. It is to be expected, then, that a large proportion of older people will see themselves as being in poor health. In a national survey of persons aged 65 and over, Ethel Shanas developed an index of illness based on interview data.[2] An illness score was computed for each respondent upon the basis of the number of diseases and physical complaints he reported, the seriousness of the complaints, and the amount of time the respondent spent in bed during the year preceding the interview. On the basis of the number of points accumulated on the illness index, old people were assigned to one of six classes. Those in classes I and II were regarded as seeing themselves as being in good health; approximately 46 per cent of those interviewed fell into this category. Respondents who fell into classes III, IV, and V were regarded as seeing themselves as being in poor health, but still able to function; approximately 44 per cent of the respondents fell into this category. The remaining 10 per cent in class VI were regarded as seeing themselves as being very sick.

It is significant that, in spite of the expectation of illness in old age, 46 per cent of the respondents in the Shanas study saw themselves as being in good health. Physical examinations would probably reveal that many of those who saw themselves as being healthy could objectively be categorized as being in poor health.

State of health is a relative matter. An old person who sees himself as being healthy at the age of 65, given the same physical condition, may have seen himself as being in poor health at 35. A significant factor in the evaluation of one's health is the reference group with which one compares oneself. The person who compares himself with his own age group, or with those older than himself, may consider himself relatively healthy even though his health actually may be impaired. On the other hand, the person who compares himself with younger people may see himself as being in poor health even though he is, in fact, relatively healthy. A person may also

[2] *The Health of Older People: A Social Survey* (Cambridge, Mass.: Harvard University Press, 1962), p. 34 ff.

use himself as a point of reference from which to evaluate the state of his health. That is, he may remember himself as he was at an earlier age and compare his present condition with his condition at that previous time. Very likely, his present condition will suffer by comparison.

Recognizing that health is not simply a physical matter and that social and psychological states must be taken into consideration, let us go on now and examine the state of health of our older population. Although it is not possible to make a clear-cut distinction between physical and mental health, we shall do so in the sections that follow to simplify discussion of health problems. The distinction between physical and mental health will be based upon diagnosis, that is, those illnesses diagnosed as physical will be treated as such and those diagnosed as mental will be treated as such.

The physical health of old people

Life expectancy has been increased through advances in medical knowledge and sanitary practices which have conquered many of the infectious diseases. The diseases that have been eliminated or controlled are those that strike people of *all* ages. The effect of these advances has been to keep people alive long enough to contract such chronic or degenerative diseases as arthritis, heart disease, and cancer—diseases that commonly strike old people.

Every year that is added to life increases the probability that the person will contract some chronic illness. According to the National Health Survey, almost four-fifths of Americans aged 65 and over are afflicted with one or more chronic illnesses, compared to fewer than two of every five persons under 35.[3] The incidence of chronic illness increases significantly with age. Among persons under 45 by 1962, 31 per cent suffered from some chronic disease; among those between 45 and 54, 57.5 per cent; among those between 55 and 64, 65 per cent; and among those 75 and over, 83.9 per cent had a chronic disease.[4] Although people aged 65 and over constituted only a little more than 9 per cent of the total noninstitutionalized population of the United States, they made up 16 per cent of those suffering from one or more chronic illnesses.

Chronic illness is not necessarily disabling, but in many cases there is some accompanying limitation of activity. It is evident from the National Health Survey that limiting effects of chronic illness are much more

[3] U.S. Department of Health, Education, and Welfare, *The Health Care of the Aged* (Washington, D.C.: U.S. Government Printing Office, 1962), p. 17.

[4] *Ibid.*, table 4, p. 18.

prevalent among old than among younger people. Of those under 65 who were reported suffering from a chronic illness, about 20 per cent experienced some limitation of activity; among those 65 and over, 56 per cent experienced at least partial limitation of activity.[5]

The specific chronic diseases from which the older persons responding to the National Health Survey most frequently reported they were suffering were arthritis and rheumatism (26.6 per cent), heart condition (14.9 per cent), and high blood pressure (12.9 per cent). It should be noted that these are diseases reported not by physicians but by the respondents themselves. Thus, there is a tendency for diseases such as cancer, which are often not detected until they reach advanced stages, to be underrepresented by the statistics. Furthermore, studies conducted by the National Health Survey have shown that chronic conditions as reported by physicians often do not match the reports given by interview respondents. The fact that the National Health Survey excluded hospitalized persons and persons who died during the study year also means that the figures reported in the study underrepresent the incidence of chronic disease among old persons.

In addition to chronic diseases, visual and hearing impairments are a serious problem among old people. Among the respondents in the National Health Survey, 17.2 per cent suffered from hearing impairments and 10.3 per cent from visual impairments.

Although chronic illness presents the most important health problem for older persons, acute illness and accidents also take their toll. In the 12-month period ending June 1959, approximately 134 acute illnesses were reported for every 100 older persons. Approximately three-fifths of the acute illnesses reported involved the respiratory system. About one of every four older persons is injured annually, and two-thirds of these accidents occur in the home. The most common types of injury are fractures, dislocations, sprains, contusions, and superficial injuries.[6]

The physical health of older persons unquestionably is a serious problem. The distressing part of it is that many of the health problems plaguing older persons could be avoided or alleviated. The difficulty arises from the fact that many older people do not get proper medical treatment. They often avoid going to physicians until it is too late. The National Health Survey found that one of every four persons aged 65 and over had not been to a physician for two years or more.[7] The regular medical checkup is not yet an accepted practice in our society—particularly among

[5] *Ibid.*
[6] *Ibid.*, p. 20.
[7] President's Council on Aging, *The Older American* (Washington, D.C.: U.S. Government Printing Office, 1963), p. 12.

older people, who are most in need of it. Then, too, people avoid going to physicians because they fear that some illness of which they are unaware will be discovered.

Older persons frequently attempt to treat themselves with patent medicines or folk remedies rather than to go to a physician. The "old, reliable doctor book" is often used for diagnosis and treatment. Or, worse yet, old wives' tales offer sure cures for almost any ailment. Quite often old people simply cannot afford medical help. Or, even if free medical help is available, the needy person may be too proud to accept charity, or the cost of transportation may be more than he can afford. Unfortunately, there is an inverse relationship between income and incidence of chronic illness. The rates of chronic illness tend to be highest among those with the most limited incomes.[8] Thus, where the need for medical care is the greatest, the ability to pay for it is most often lacking.

The health problems of some older persons stem from the fact that they do not eat properly. They are intrigued by food fads, they have poor eating habits, they do not bother to eat regularly, or they cannot afford to eat regularly and properly. Proper nutrition could be the solution to many of the health problems experienced by old people. Departments of public health are currently engaged in research and education projects designed to improve the eating habits of older persons.[9] However, the habits of a lifetime are very difficult to change.

The mental health of old people

Contrary to popular belief, serious mental impairment is not an inevitable consequence of aging. Many famous scientists and artists have made their major contributions at advanced ages. For a large proportion of older people, there is no discernible deterioration of the mental processes. Nevertheless, mental health presents a serious problem for the elderly.

Approximately 1 per cent of Americans aged 65 or over are in mental hospitals. Of course, many others who have been or could be diagnosed as mentally ill are not hospitalized. The seriousness of the mental health problem for old people is emphasized by the fact that although they represent only a little more than 9 per cent of the total population, persons

[8] Special Committee on Aging, United States Senate, *Basic Facts on The Health and Economic Status of Older Americans* (Washington, D.C.: U.S. Government Printing Office, 1961), p. 1.

[9] Marian Emerson, *Changing the Dietary Behavior of Older Adults*, An Experimental Health Education Program Authorized by the California State Department of Public Health for the City of Pasadena, Project No. 0102, 1965.

aged 65 and over represent 27 per cent of the first admissions to public mental hospitals.[10] This first-admission rate is more than two and a half times as high as the rate for younger people.[11] According to an American Hospital Association estimate, one-third of the patient population in mental hospitals is in the 65-and-over age group.[12] Many of these persons, however, have grown old within the confines of the hospital.

Among first admissions to mental hospitals, schizophrenia and manic-depressive psychoses are the most frequent diagnoses among young adults; involutional, alcoholic, and syphilitic psychoses are most common among the middle-aged; and organic brain damage is most common among elderly people.[13] By the age of 70, 27 per cent of all first admissions are attributed to brain damage. Circulatory difficulties are the leading source of brain damage. For instance, stroke interrupts the normal supply of blood to the brain and results in damage to the organ. Arteriosclerosis also results in impaired flow of blood to the brain and, therefore, in brain damage.[14] Senile brain disease is another major source of brain damage among old people. Through a process not yet fully understood, there is a wasting away of the brain substance itself.[15]

Although victims of organic brain damage represent the largest number of first admissions to mental hospitals among old people, such patients constitute just 12 per cent of the total patient population. The largest proportion of patients in mental hospitals are diagnosed as schizophrenics (46 per cent). These persons enter the hospitals young and stay for long periods (an average of 10.5 years). On the other hand, the average length of stay for senile patients is 2.4 years. Many of these senile patients die soon after admission, an estimated 70 per cent.[16]

Although the so-called functional disorders (those with no evidence of brain damage) are more characteristic of younger patients, old people are by no means immune to them. The onset of schizophrenia and the manic-depressive psychoses may occur at any point in life. There is some reason to believe that there is a relationship between social isolation and the incidence of schizophrenia.[17] However, it is not possible to say at this time

[10] President's Council on Aging, *On Growing Older* (Washington, D.C.: U.S. Government Printing Office, 1964), pp. 59–60.

[11] Special Committee on Aging, United States Senate, *Developments in Aging: 1959 to 1963* (Washington, D.C.: U.S. Government Printing Office, 1963), p. 5.

[12] *Ibid.*, p. 6.

[13] Eugene A. Confrey and Marcus S. Goldstein, "The Health Status of Aging People," in Clark Tibbitts, ed., *Handbook of Social Gerontology: Societal Aspects of Aging* (Chicago: The University of Chicago Press, 1960), p. 182.

[14] President's Council on Aging, *On Growing Older*, p. 60.

[15] *Ibid.*

[16] Confrey and Goldstein, *op. cit.*, p. 182.

[17] Robert E. L. Faris and H. Warren Dunham, *Mental Disorders in Urban Areas* (New York: Hafner, 1960).

what the nature of the relationship is. They do frequently appear together, however. Since social isolation is not uncommon among older persons, particularly after the deaths of spouses and peers, it is not surprising to find cases of schizophrenia among the elderly. Neither is it unusual to find cases of depression among older persons. Such traumatic events as the death of a spouse, retirement, or serious physical illness are often accompanied by periods of depression. It is significant that a very large proportion of older people entering mental hospitals with diagnoses of functional disorders are also suffering from chronic physical disorders.

It cannot be assumed that the old people in mental hospitals are necessarily more ill than those not hospitalized. Nor can it be assumed that those in hospitals could not be cared for outside. In fact, one study indicated that more than 50 per cent of the patients aged 60 or over in state mental hospitals could be cared for outside the hospital confines.[18] Rather than extent of illness, it is often the social situation in which an old person lives which determines whether he will be committed to a mental hospital. An old person who lives alone and has no close relatives may end up in a hospital because there is no one to care for him. But many of those who do have families end up in mental hospitals because their families cannot, or will not, care for them. Children with families of their own may be unable to devote the time necessary to care for grandparents. In other cases, relatives may feel that it is not their responsibility to care for the old folks. Committing the old person to a mental hospital is a tempting way to get him out from under foot. The Philadelphia Mental Health Survey Committee in 1954 sent a questionnaire to officials in charge of mental hospitals and to psychiatrists working with mental hospitals. Of the 50 respondents to the questionnaire, 16 estimated that between 10 and 75 per cent of the patients admitted to mental hospitals for senility were, in fact, not psychotic.[19]

Economic aspects of the health problem

Given the fact that older persons have higher rates of illness than younger ones, it follows that they make greater use of health services. According to the National Health Survey, persons aged 65 and over average 6.8 visits to physicians per year, compared to 4.8 visits for persons under 65.[20] One of every six older persons goes into a hospital each year.

[18] Confrey and Goldstein, *op. cit.*, p. 183.
[19] *Ibid.*
[20] U.S. Department of Health, Education, and Welfare, *Health Care of the Aged*, p. 23.

Furthermore, the average hospital stay is two weeks—twice as long as the average stay for younger persons. The older person's hospital bill is generally twice as large.[21] Of those hospitalized during the two-year period ending June 1960, 19 per cent were in the hospital from 15 to 30 days per year and 9 per cent, more than 31 days.[22]

Since the National Health Survey data excluded persons who had died in the year preceding the survey, the figures given on hospital utilization undoubtedly underestimate the actual rates. It has been estimated that if the National Health Survey had included those who had died during the survey year, the number of days of hospital care of older persons would have been increased by 40 per cent.[23]

Nursing homes and other long-term institutions are largely populated by older persons. The average age of patients in many nursing homes is as high as 80.[24] It has been estimated that older persons constitute roughly 33 per cent of the patients in mental hospitals, 20 per cent of those in tuberculosis hospitals, and about 50 per cent of those in other long-term institutions.[25]

Older persons are much more likely to require home care of some kind than are younger persons. Ethel Shanas has estimated that 7 to 8 per cent of the elderly are either bedridden or housebound. Of the ambulatory aged, she estimates that approximately 30 per cent have difficulty walking stairs, 10 per cent have difficulty bathing, 8 per cent have difficulty dressing, and 20 per cent have difficulty cutting their toenails.[26]

It may seem a little surprising that cutting one's toenails can constitute a health problem, but it is true. Many older people experience a thickening of the nails as a result of fungus infection. These thickened nails can cause much discomfort, inconvenience, and danger of infection. Departments of public health have come to recognize this problem and are now making provisions for health workers to care for the toenails of elderly people. The amount of full-time or part-time home care increases with age. Persons 65 and over are fifteen times as likely as younger people to receive some kind of home care.[27]

The only health service older people utilize less than young people is dental care. Persons aged 65 and over make only about half as many visits

[21] President's Council on Aging, *The Older American*, p. 14.
[22] U.S. Department of Health, Education, and Welfare, *Health Care of the Aged*, p. 25.
[23] *Ibid.*, footnote, p. 28.
[24] *Ibid.*, p. 29.
[25] *Ibid.*, p. 31.
[26] "Health Problems of the Aged," paper presented at the annual meetings of the Western Gerontological Society, Los Angeles, Calif., November 13, 1965.
[27] U.S. Department of Health, Education, and Welfare, *Health Care of the Aged*, p. 31.

to dentists per year as younger persons. Undoubtedly, many older persons feel that, once their teeth have been extracted and they have been fitted with dentures, the necessity for visits to a dentist ceases. Of course this is not the case. Dentures need to be checked periodically for proper fit. As a result of their failure to make regular visits to dentists, a great number of older persons suffer annoying denture problems which may be related to poor diet.

The medical expenses of older people are substantially higher than those of younger people. In 1961, the average medical expenses paid from private funds by persons aged 65 or over were $226, compared to $103 for persons under 65. Of the $226, $77 went to pay for hospital care and the other $149 for all other medical expenses, including nursing-home care. Those older persons who were hospitalized during the year paid an average hospital bill —not including their doctors' fees and other expenses—of about $525.[28]

Of a total of 24.5 billion dollars of public and private expenditures for medical care for the entire population in 1960, about 5 billion dollars was spent for the medical care of older persons. In other words, although the 65-and-over age category constituted only a little more than 9 per cent of the population, approximately 20 per cent of the expenditure for medical care was for older people. The major share of the costs of medical care for older people is paid from private funds. About 72 per cent of the total was paid either by the older people themselves or by their friends or relatives.[29]

The older person with a relatively fixed income is the victim of spiraling medical costs. In the period during which the Department of Labor's Consumer Price Index was increasing by 26 per cent, overall medical costs increased 56 per cent, doctors' fees 47 per cent, and the daily charges for hospital care 125 per cent.[30]

The major medical crisis facing the older person is the need for hospitalization. This need often comes up without adequate warning, requiring large financial outlays that are difficult to anticipate. Adding to the problem is the fact that hospital bills must be paid all at once. Many older persons, living on limited incomes, hope against hope that they will not become ill enough to require hospitalization. However, some hospitalization is almost inevitable. It has been estimated that 9 of every 10 persons aged 65 or over will be hospitalized at least once in their remaining lifetimes; moreover, 2 of every 3 will be hospitalized more than once.[31]

[28] President's Council on Aging, *The Older American*, pp. 14–15.
[29] U.S. Department of Health, Education, and Welfare, *Health Care of the Aged*, p. 33.
[30] President's Council on Aging, *The Older American*, p. 15.
[31] U.S. Department of Health, Education, and Welfare, *Health Care of the Aged*, p. 39.

According to the National Health Survey, of all elderly persons not in institutions in 1960–61, 46 per cent had some kind of hospital insurance, 37 per cent had surgical insurance, and 10 per cent had insurance covering doctors' visits.[32] However, a deceptive aspect of the private medical plan picture is the extent to which costs are covered. In a survey conducted of all elderly persons discharged from short-term hospitals between July 1958 and June 1960, it was found that in almost 50 per cent of the cases health insurance covered no part of the bill, and in about 30 per cent of the cases only 75 per cent of the cost.[33] Adequate private health insurance coverage for an older couple would cost at least $400 per year. This amounts to about one-sixth of the total annual income of the average elderly couple.[34] Almost three-fourths of the older families in the United States in 1960 were two-person families, for whom the median income was $2,530.[35]

The significant economic fact about the health problems of older persons is that, whereas their medical costs run twice as high as those of younger people, their incomes are only half as large. Only a relatively small proportion of older persons do have substantial incomes and are able to afford ordinary medical costs. However, major medical crises involving long hospitalization can soon exhaust presumably adequate financial resources. Cooley and Cooley report the case of a 68-year-old man whose $168,000 estate was practically wiped out by a siege of cancer.[36] The overwhelming majority of older persons do not have adequate financial resources to cover medical emergencies. Those with the most limited resources are also those with the highest rates of illness.

Social aspects of the health problem

With the steady increase in the number of persons aged 65 and older, the health of older persons will be an increasing problem. More old people in the population means more sick people. The problem of meeting the medical needs of older people cannot be wished away; it is here to stay.

Who is responsible for caring for the needs of older people? Shanas asked a sample of older people, a sample of individuals responsible for older people, and a cross section of the population: "Who do you think should take care of older people when they are no longer working?" Of the

[32] *Ibid.*, p. 62.
[33] *Ibid.*, p. 63.
[34] President's Council on Aging, *The Older American*, p. 19.
[35] U.S. Department of Health, Education, and Welfare, *Health Care of the Aged*, p. 44.
[36] Leland F. Cooley and Lee M. Cooley, *The Retirement Trap* (Garden City, N.Y.: Doubleday & Company, Inc., 1965), p. 2.

older people, about 24 per cent felt that they should provide for themselves, 26 per cent that children or relatives should care for them, and 41 per cent that the government should shoulder the responsibility. Among the individuals responsible for older persons, 18 per cent felt that the older people should take care of themselves, 40 per cent that children or relatives should be responsible, and 34 per cent that the government should be responsible. Of the cross section of the population, 17 per cent felt that older persons should provide for themselves, 33 per cent that children or relatives should provide for them, and 43 per cent that the government should provide for them.[37]

Older persons seldom like to feel dependent upon their children or relatives; nor are they willing to accept charity. They will accept government aid if it is presented to them in the form of insurance rather than charity. The 41 per cent in Shanas' sample who felt that the government should shoulder the responsibility for their care were undoubtedly thinking of social security benefits, which are usually considered insurance rather than charity.

Although a sizable percentage of the responsible individuals felt that they should provide for their elderly, it is safe to say that Americans generally do not feel the same degree of personal responsibility for the older members of their families as do persons in other societies. In countries such as China and Japan, neglect of one's duty to one's elders leads irrevocably to disgrace. Among Americans, elderly persons do not enjoy the same degree of respect and deference as they do in the Orient. Most persons feel some degree of responsibility toward their elders, but under certain conditions other responsibilities take priority. For example, in choosing between the needs of his immediate family and the needs of his parents, the American man is likely to think first about his immediate family. Shanas says:

A majority of older people and of the public believe that adult sons and daughters must assume certain responsibilities toward aged parents. These responsibilities of children to parents are largely in the area of interpersonal relationships. Most persons, whether old or young, feel that sons and daughters should be willing to make adjustments in their mode of life when self-interest conflicts with the needs and interests of aging parents. While a substantial group among the sons and daughters of older people share this point of view, a majority do not always agree that "parents come first." Apparently, the children of older people are strongly motivated to maintain good relationships with their parents if it is at all possible, but the demands and needs of their own families sometimes conflict with and override their parents' demands and needs.[38]

[37] *The Health of Older People,* table 81, p. 133.
[38] *Ibid.,* p. 141.

It is interesting to note that the most frequent response among all three groups studied by Shanas was that the government should be responsible for the care of older persons. It was probably in response to such sentiment that the Medicare Program became law in 1965. Though it promised to offer some needed help to older people in meeting the costs of their medical care, the Medicare plan is certainly not adequate to solve the health problems of the elderly. Significantly, about one-third of those older persons who elected not to sign up for the supplementary part of the Medicare Program, designed to provide partial payment of doctors' bills and other expenses, said that they could not afford to pay even $3 a month for the added benefits.[39]

There is a definite relationship between the state of a person's health and his feelings of dignity and self-respect. Older persons who feel rejected or neglected are more likely to see their health as being poor than those who are accepted. There is an unfortunate distrust of and distaste for old age and old people in our society. It is no wonder that, under such circumstances, many of our older people are desolate, depressed, and sick. The problem is much deeper than the physical problems of health. It is a problem whose solution lies more properly in some basic changes in the American value system. Recognition of the fact that ever larger numbers of our citizens will be among the elderly and assignment to them of a respected place in our social system, could do much to alleviate their health problems—particularly the problem of mental health.

[39] Los Angeles *Herald-Examiner*, December 20, 1965.

Chapter 4. Housing

SUITABLE living accommodations are necessary for the well-being of people of all ages and stations in life. However, the suitability of living accommodations becomes even more crucial for older persons, because of the proportionately greater amount of time they are likely to spend at home. Some older people spend almost every moment of their last years at home. As the United States Senate's Special Committee on Aging has pointed out,

> Housing and its immediate physical surroundings influence well-being and the quality of life of people in any age group, but suitable housing is doubly important to the retired person whose home is the center of virtually all of his activities. Few factors have as much potential for promoting the well-being of the elderly as housing of appropriate size which offers safety, comfort, and the opportunity of choice between privacy and contact with the community.[1]

Living accommodations are an even more central concern for old people than they are for young people because (1) old people spend more time at home, and (2) old people tend to be more socially isolated. There is some evidence that social isolation leads to increased concern over physical facilities such as housing. Whereas people who are socially integrated tend to express concern about the quality of their social relationships, people who are socially isolated tend to express correspondingly more concern about the quality of their physical facilities.[2]

Housing that may be perfectly adequate for the young may not suit the needs of the elderly. Most older families are two-person families, consisting of husband and wife. They need less space and find that the house in which they raised their families becomes a drain upon their energies once the children have left home. The older couple may, therefore, desire to move to a smaller house or an apartment whose maintenance cost is lower. But the proceeds of the sale of the "old house" may be inadequate for purchase of a newer, smaller dwelling.

[1] *Developments in Aging: 1963 and 1964*, Report No. 124 (Washington, D.C.: U.S. Government Printing Office, 1965), p. 29.

[2] Edward Gross, Herman J. Loether, Duane N. Strinden, and L. Wes Wager, *A Study of Cohesion in the Small Group;* Final Report, Phase II, U.S. Air Force Archives, Randolph Air Force Base, Randolph Field, Texas, 1953, pp. 153–156.

Aside from space, other factors must be considered in evaluating the adequacy of housing for the elderly. Old people tend to become less mobile, and the proximity of their housing to shopping centers, churches, medical services, recreational facilities, and other amenities becomes important. If such facilities are not within easy walking distance, adequate low-cost public transportation must be available.

Older persons who do not do their own cooking and do not have accommodations that include food services tend to be concentrated in areas where restaurants and cafeterias serving moderately priced meals are found. Cafeterias are especially popular, because they offer maximum flexibility in the selection of food and eliminate the necessity of tipping. In Pasadena, California, a city noted for its concentration of old people, the census tract with the greatest concentration of old people is in an area with a wide assortment of stores, restaurants, cafeterias, churches, and easily accessible public transportation.

The design features housing experts consider desirable and generally recommend in the construction of housing for the elderly are:

1. An adequate system of temperature and climate control. Older persons often require more warmth than young people to be comfortable. For this reason an efficient heating system with thermostatic control, a weather-proof unit free from drafts, and a system of humidity control are considered highly desirable. In those parts of the country where summers are excessively warm, air-conditioning units are recommended.

2. Adequate sources of both sunlight and artificial light. Older people frequently have difficulty in seeing and require greater light intensity than the young.

3. Adequate control of sound and noise. Although excessive noise can be a source of irritation to old people, excessive quiet can be equally disturbing. It is desirable to design housing for the elderly in such a way as to keep noise and sound levels within the acceptable range. Persons who have difficulty in hearing should be provided with amplifying systems for door bells, telephones, radios, television sets, and so forth.

4. Efficient design of the housing unit should assure the maximum conservation of energy and minimize the necessity for reaching, lifting, bending, pulling, and climbing. Though a moderate amount of exercise can be beneficial, it is desirable to avoid excessive exertion. Some of the units built for older residents include electric plugs placed a little higher than usual, light switches placed low enough to be reached from a wheelchair, railings and support bars placed in strategic places, halls and doorways wide enough for wheelchairs, and access ramps as well as stairs.

5. Safety factors should be built into housing units for older persons. The old are more accident prone than young people, and most of their

accidents occur in the home. The most common home accidents among old people are falls. Next are accidents associated with fires. It is important to design housing facilities for the elderly that will protect them against falls, fires, and other hazards.[3]

Though these recommended design features are important to the well-being of our older citizens, they need not be limited to good housing for the elderly. They could well be incorporated into all new housing units and be of benefit to residents of all ages.

Types of accommodations

The widely varied housing needs and preferences of our 65-and-over population are reflected in the variety of accommodations in which they are found. The majority of older persons prefer to live in homes of their own, but they differ considerably in the specifics of their housing preferences. Furthermore, for many older persons there is considerable disparity between their housing preferences and the actual circumstances in which they live.

In a national survey of persons aged 65 and over conducted in 1957, Ethel Shanas found that 83.3 per cent of the respondents preferred to live in their own homes, 7.5 per cent with a child or relative, and 2.9 per cent in a home for the aged.[4]

A California study found that about 2 of every 3 persons 65 and over maintained their own households, either living with a spouse or alone; almost 1 of every 4 lived with an adult child; and about 1 of every 10 lived with some other relative.[5] The California State Department of Social Welfare surveyed the living accommodations of 250,000 Old Age Security recipients in 1956.[6] It was found that 61.3 per cent of the respondents lived in houses, 23.3 per cent in apartments or flats, 2.5 per cent in hotels, 4 per cent in rooming houses, 0.3 per cent in boarding houses, 4.2 per cent in boarding or rest homes, and 0.9 per cent in institutions. These California data are comparable to those for the nation as a whole.

Most older people live in houses, apartments, or flats; however, many of

[3] Walter K. Vivrett, "Housing and Community Settings for Older People," in Clark Tibbitts, ed., *Handbook of Social Gerontology: Societal Aspects of Aging* (Chicago: The University of Chicago Press, 1960), pp. 585–586.

[4] *The Health of Older People: A Social Survey* (Cambridge, Mass.: Harvard University Press, 1962), table 64, p. 103.

[5] *California Legislature Report of the Senate Subcommittee on Housing and Recreational Needs of Elderly Citizens.* Published by the Senate of the State of California, 1961, pp. 30–31.

[6] *Ibid.*, p. 32.

these units are substandard. Of the people aged 65 and over who are heads of households, about 30 per cent live in dwelling units that are judged to be substandard. In 1960, 26 per cent of owner-occupied and 40 per cent of renter-occupied units were rated as deficient in some respect. The Census Bureau classifies as deficient units that are dilapidated, deteriorated, or lacking in some or all of the plumbing facilities.[7] In a study of social security recipients it was found that 80 per cent were living in houses at least 30 years old and 40 per cent, in houses at least 51 years old.[8] There is no question that there is a serious problem of housing our aged population adequately.

In the past few years, a number of different types of specialized facilities have been developed to help meet the housing needs of the elderly. Prominent among these are the so-called retirement communities. These developments consist of houses or apartments that are sold to families without minor children whose head is beyond some minimum age—usually 50. Many of these communities are almost self-contained. They include shopping centers, churches, restaurants, recreation centers, golf courses, swimming pools, and—occasionally—medical centers. There are no schools! The prices of the dwelling units typically are in the $10,000–$20,000 range. In addition, there may be a monthly maintenance fee and yearly dues for membership in the community recreation center. Retirement communities of this type have sprung up in the warm, sunny climates of Arizona, California, and Florida and have attracted residents from all parts of the country through national advertising campaigns. Usually, when all the units are sold out, the developer turns the management of the community over to its residents.

Another development in housing for the aged is the deluxe, high-rise apartment building in the central city. While the retirement community requires large areas of land for development and is usually found on the outskirts of metropolitan areas, the relatively small land requirements of an apartment building make it possible to locate it in the heart of the city. Individual units in the apartment building may be either rented or sold; some buildings have both rental and sale units available. Frequently, restaurants or central dining rooms are included in the building for the use of the residents. Recreational facilities and small shops featuring personal services and specialty items are usually an integral part of the building complex. The apartment building complexes are generally not self-contained, as the retirement communities are, because they are not as isolated. The selling point of the apartment buildings is that they are centrally

[7] President's Council on Aging, *The Older American* (Washington, D.C.: U.S. Government Printing Office, 1963), pp. 24–25.
[8] *Ibid.*, p. 24.

located, so that all of the facilities of the city are available to the residents.

Another concept in housing the elderly is the mobile home park. Mobile home parks, common in Florida, Arizona, and California, rent trailer space to the elderly at a monthly rate that includes utilities and laundry, toilet, and recreational facilities. Frequently, the management of the park will carry on an organized social and recreational program for the benefit of the residents. Originally, the mobile home parks were attractive to older people because of the mobility of trailer living. However, many residents of these facilities build permanent patios and porches onto their trailers, eliminating the mobility factor. Some of the mobile homes now being sold are almost as big and elaborate as houses and not much more mobile. They are moved only once, from the sales lot to the mobile home park.

The advantage the mobile home enjoys over the house is a tax break. Mobile homes are taxed as vehicles rather than as dwelling units, thus providing a substantial savings in taxes. They also may afford the advantage of low maintenance costs and compactness.

A number of church groups sponsor homes for the aged. Most of these homes offer modest living accommodations, but a few are very elaborate. Some provide suites of rooms and others feature detached units. These homes generally offer a life-care arrangement in which the tenant pays a founders' fee upon moving in and then pays monthly rent. Founders' fees vary from a few hundred dollars to as much as $30,000. These fees are used to cover capital costs, to defray the cost of services to the residents, and to subsidize those residents unable to pay the full monthly rent.[9] The founders' fee and monthly rent are based on the tenant's average life expectancy according to actuarial tables. The founders' fee may also entitle the resident to medical care.

In August 1963, the Housing and Home Finance Agency of the federal government issued a regulation requiring the sponsoring agency offering life-care contracts to provide legally enforceable guarantees of lifetime care to the residents.[10] This regulation was enacted to protect residents against the possibility of financial failure by homes for the aged. In the past, residents who put their life savings into founders' fees have been left high and dry—with neither their money nor their life care—when homes without sound financial backing failed.

Many older hotels, no longer able to compete for the transient hotel trade, have begun to offer permanent accommodations to the elderly at modest prices. Also, a few corporations have gone into the business of

[9] Special Committee on Aging, United States Senate, *Developments in Aging: 1963 and 1964*, p. 31.

[10] *Ibid.*, p. 56.

providing such accommodations. These corporations buy up older hotels in downtown areas, equip them with some recreational facilities and services for the elderly, and rent rooms on the American plan (with meals) for as little as $60 a month. Like the deluxe apartment building, these hotels have the advantage of being centrally located within easy walking distance of a great number of amenities attractive to the elderly.

Big, old houses, deteriorated with age and now located in transitional areas of the city, are often turned into boarding houses or housekeeping rooms for the elderly. Frequently, landlords rent these facilities at very modest prices during the transitional period of the neighborhood. Rather than renovating the building, the owner rents rooms for what he can get and holds on to the property, until industry or multiple dwellings invade the area. Then he sells the property for the land value and realizes a handsome profit. These older, transitional neighborhoods with boarding houses and housekeeping rooms have large concentrations of older people living on limited retirement incomes.

The Housing Act of 1937, designed to provide low-rent public housing, was amended by the United States Congress in 1956 to authorize the construction of housing units especially for the elderly. The Congressional action of 1956 also made it possible for single elderly persons to occupy public housing; previously, public housing had been available only to families. By the end of 1964, approximately 80,900 public housing units were earmarked expressly for the elderly. These units provide modest living accommodations for the older person or family at a minimal rent based upon the ability to pay. The median rent charged for public housing units for the elderly during the first half of 1964 was $33 a month, including utilities.[11]

Although a relatively small proportion of our older population needs institutionalized care (Shanas estimated it at 4 per cent[12]), about 88 per cent of persons living in nursing and personal-care homes are 65 or over.[13] In 1963, there were about 445,500 persons 65 or over in some 16,370 nursing or personal-care homes in the United States. Homes that provided nursing care as their primary service constituted 48 per cent of the total; homes giving primarily personal care with some nursing service, 30 per cent; and homes providing personal care only, the remaining 22 per cent.

[11] *Ibid.*, p. 30.
[12] Ethel Shanas, "Health Problems of the Aged." paper presented at the annual meeting of the Western Gerontological Society, Los Angeles, Calif., November 13, 1965.
[13] Public Health Service, U.S. Department of Health, Education, and Welfare, *Characteristics of Residents in Institutions for the Aged and Chronically Ill: United States, April–June 1963*, National Center for Health Statistics, Series 12, No. 2 (Washington, D.C.: U.S. Government Printing Office, 1965), p. 3.

Whereas the nursing-care and the personal-care-with-nursing homes averaged about 40 beds, the smaller personal-care homes averaged 16 beds. Of these homes, 82 per cent were privately owned and operated, 12 per cent by nonprofit organizations, and the remaining 6 per cent by local and state governments or the federal government. Although the privately owned homes constituted 82 per cent of the total number, they accounted for only 61 per cent of the residents because they were generally smaller.[14]

The quality and cost of services in nursing and personal-care homes vary tremendously. Some homes, run with inadequate staffs, offer barely minimal care to residents. Necessary equipment may also be lacking, and the building may be dilapidated and unsafe. Grisly tales may be told about the conditions found in many such homes. Other homes have excellent staffs, modern equipment, and efficiently designed buildings.

Many operators of privately owned nursing homes realize handsome profits on their investments. In some cases the annual returns have been as high as 20 or 30 per cent of the investment. In Southern California many eager, but inexperienced, investors plunged into the nursing home "business" in the mid-60's in the hope of making a killing from the allowances provided by California's Medical Assistance to the Aged program and the Medicare program. As a result, more nursing homes were constructed than were needed, and the average vacancy rate rose to 30 per cent. Many of those who expected to get rich quick instead found themselves bankrupt.[15]

There has been much concern over the quality of care old people have received in nursing and personal-care homes. Investigations have been conducted by units of the local, state, and federal governments, and steps have been taken to raise the minimum standards of care provided. Regardless of the quality of established standards, the problem of enforcement remains. The Medicare Program set high standards of care for nursing homes to meet before they might qualify for reimbursement of costs. This is a step in the right direction, but there is no question that more needs to be done.

Economic aspects of housing problems

In a study of the housing problems of the elderly that he conducted in Cleveland, Irving Rosow found that those who were most dissatisfied with their housing were in the low-income brackets. He concluded that the

[14] *Ibid.*, pp. 2–3.
[15] Los Angeles *Times*, February 13, 1966.

housing problems of the elderly derive basically from economic problems.[16]

On the average, the older family's income is only about half as large as that of the younger family. As a result, the older family is forced to spend a greater percentage of income for housing. Nevertheless, the amount the older family spends on housing is considerably less than that spent by the younger family. Consequently, the older family is more likely to be housed in substandard accommodations. It has been estimated that about 5 million elderly persons and couples are occupying unsuitable housing. In 1960, nearly two and three-quarter million households headed by persons 65 and over lived in deficient quarters. Elderly families are twice as likely as younger families to be living in deficient structures.[17]

Even when they own their own homes, mortgage free, elderly families are faced with rising property taxes, insurance, and maintenance costs. Maintenance costs are correspondingly higher for elderly than for younger people because (1) the older people require more help in maintaining their property, and (2) the overwhelming majority of older homeowners are living in houses 30 or more years old, and these houses generally are more in need of repairs than those built more recently.

The low-cost housing available to older people is frequently substandard. The boarding houses, housekeeping rooms, and hotel rooms available to them are often old and dilapidated and located in deteriorating neighborhoods. Many older people will accept substandard accommodations without complaint because they are happy to find any accommodations they can afford. There have been numerous tragic incidents in which elderly people have lost their lives in fires due directly or indirectly to the dilapidated conditions of boarding houses or hotels in which they were living.

Public housing helps meet the needs of some older families in the low-income brackets, but there is not enough of it available to meet the demand. Even when such housing is available, its location in low-income areas, with their high rate of lawlessness, discourages the aged from accepting the low-cost quarters at the price of possible danger. Furthermore, public housing is available only to those with very limited incomes. Many older people cannot qualify for public housing, but still have incomes too limited to cover the costs of adequate housing of other kinds.

There has been a great boom in the construction of housing for the elderly in retirement communities, but these homes and apartments are too costly for the bulk of the older population. Of the residents of Sun

[16] "Housing the Aged," paper presented at the annual meetings of the Western Gerontological Society, Los Angeles, Calif., November 13, 1965.
[17] Special Committee on Aging, United States Senate, *Developments in Aging: 1963 and 1964*, p. 29.

City, Arizona, about one-third had incomes of $12,000 or more a year before retirement, and another third had incomes between $8,000 to $12,000. Sixty-two per cent of the residents were able to pay cash for their retirement homes, which ranged in price from $10,450 to $15,950.[18]

James A. Peterson and Aili E. Larson, in a study of Laguna Hills Leisure World, in Southern California, found that 55.4 per cent of the residents had been engaged in professional or managerial occupations before retirement, compared to about 25.3 per cent of the California population at large. Also, 45 per cent of the residents had attended college, compared to about 16 per cent of the general population.[19]

Because of the cost factor, therefore, the retirement communities being built are available to only a small proportion of the elderly. The Special Committee on Aging set up by the United States Senate showed some concern over the possibility that such units might be overbuilt. A report published by the Committee says:

The almost explosive growth of retirement community development gives rise to concern on several counts. The first of these relates to the actual demand for retirement community housing. The market for housing in age-limited retirement communities is a specialized and limited market and there has been little effort to measure its size. Moreover, the number of units in retirement communities in existence and under development is not known . . .

Any substantial number of failures among such developments would be a serious problem in itself, but of still greater concern are the catastrophic consequences to the older people who had invested and were stranded in partially developed and bankrupt communities. Nearby communities or county governments would find heavy demands upon them to provide lacking facilities and services for the hapless elderly residents caught in these situations.[20]

It is certain that retirement communities will not meet the needs of the average older person. The older people whose housing needs are being met most inadequately are those who have moderate incomes—too high to qualify for public housing, but not high enough to allow them to take advantage of privately sponsored developments. It is in this area that the development of housing units for the elderly is sorely lacking.

As concern over the housing needs of the elderly has increased, the federal government has been taking an ever more active role. A number of aid programs are currently in operation:

[18] Calvin Trillin, "A Reporter at Large: Wake Up and Live," *The New Yorker*, XL, No. 7 (April 4, 1964), pp. 133, 136.
[19] "Socio-Psychological Factors in Selecting Retirement Housing," revised version of paper read at the Research Conference on Patterns of Living and Housing of Middle-Aged and Older People, Washington, D.C., March 1965, pp. 8–9.
[20] *Developments in Aging: 1963 and 1964*, pp. 38–39.

1. The federal government encourages the development of low-rent, public housing in which provision is made for a certain proportion of elderly residents. Public housing units planned, built, and operated by local housing authorities are subsidized by the federal government.

2. The Federal Housing Authority is authorized to insure lenders against losses on mortgages used for the construction or rehabilitation of rental units for older people. This program is designed to encourage private financing for private, profit-motivated builders, nonprofit organizations, and government units.

3. The Community Facilities Administration of the federal government is authorized to make direct loans to nonprofit organizations to build new rental housing for the elderly. These are long-term, low-interest loans.

4. The Federal Housing Authority is authorized to insure a lender against losses on a mortgage for housing being purchased by a person 62 years old or older. Furthermore, it is permissible for a relative, friend, or corporation to make a down payment for the elderly purchaser. The elderly person unable to qualify for a loan himself may qualify by obtaining a co-signer. This program is designed to make it possible for more elderly people to buy homes of their own, because in the past it has been practically impossible for an elderly purchaser to obtain a mortgage.

5. In addition, there are a number of federal programs designed to assist elderly residents of rural areas to find adequate housing. These programs include mortgage insurance, direct loans to nonprofit organizations, and financial assistance to the elderly persons themselves.[21]

Although the many federal programs are helpful, they do not solve the housing problems of the elderly. The solution to these problems is still one of the great challenges of our times.

Social aspects of housing problems

There is no doubt that the economic problems of the aged aggravate their housing problems. Equally important, however, are the social aspects of their housing problems. Successful interpersonal relations can be crucial to successful housing. Of course, people differ widely in the extent to which they are dependent upon interpersonal relations. Some people prefer to be alone and get along perfectly well on their own; others need much social interaction in order to be content. Every person should have the

[21] Special Committee on Aging, United States Senate, *Developments in Aging: 1959 to 1963* (Washington, D.C.: U.S. Government Printing Office, 1963), pp. 99–105.

opportunity to enjoy the amount and quality of interpersonal relations necessary to meet his needs.

Older people, ordinarily, prefer to live alone rather than with children or other relatives. However, the elderly sometimes have no alternative. More than 2 million elderly persons or couples live with children or other relatives.[22] The fact that most older people prefer not to live with children or other relatives should not be construed as a desire to avoid interpersonal relations with them. Generally, the elderly prefer to maintain their own households, but to live near enough to children and relatives so that they can visit them and call upon them when they need help; but they would rather not share the same accommodations. Some older people do not wish to be a burden to their relatives. Others feel that they maintain their independence as long as they have their own households. Still others feel that they would not be able to adjust to an intergenerational living situation. Although most grandparents enjoy their grandchildren, they may prefer to enjoy them *occasionally* at close range, but *generally* at long range.

Many older people who live with relatives find their accommodations unsatisfactory because of insufficient living space and a lack of opportunity for privacy and individual activities. No matter how well elderly parents get along with their children and grandchildren, if there is not enough available living space, the situation is likely to be something less than pleasant. Everybody needs some breathing room and a little space to call his own.

There is some debate whether it is more desirable for older people to be integrated into communities with people of all ages or whether it is preferable for them to locate in such age-segregated settings as the retirement communities. Those who advocate the age-segregated communities as most desirable argue that the elderly are most happy with people of their own age; they have common interests and perspectives that make for satisfying interpersonal relations. It is also argued that older people are uncomfortable around younger people and irritated by children and are happiest away from the commotion, in a relaxed atmosphere where they are free to do as they like. Those who argue in favor of the integrated community say that it is a more natural situation. Being around young people keeps one young; those who associate with the old become old themselves.

Most older people do not seek out age-segregated communities. They prefer to stay in their own homes in their own neighborhoods rather than move to retirement communities. Nevertheless, a natural kind of age-

[22] Special Committee on Aging, United States Senate, *Developments in Aging: 1963 and 1964*, p. 29.

segregation often tends to develop in those neighborhoods where older people live. The houses become older and the children grow up and leave, but they are not replaced by other children. Eventually the neighborhood comes to be inhabited almost exclusively by older people.

Those older people who do choose to move to age-segregated communities generally seem to be satisfied with them. It has been estimated that as many as 95 per cent of retirement-community residents are happy with their lot. They enjoy the facilities available to them and their interpersonal relations with other residents. Some contend that they are busier than they have ever been before.

It is exactly this busyness to which some of the dissenters object. They say that retirement-community living is a sham. Retirement-community inhabitants seem to frantically keep busy at unimportant activities in order to avoid facing up to the fact that they are old and do not have much time left. Those who criticize the constant round of activities feel that there are much more important and more profitable ways for the elderly to make use of their time than card parties, shuffleboard games, or ceramics classes. In addition, many people find a community composed entirely of elderly people depressing; they say that there is the smell of death in the air. And, it must be admitted, death is ever present and frequently highly visible in these age-segregated communities. The Grim Reaper frequently reminds those who are frantically participating in the advertised "101 social and recreational activities" that they have an inevitable appointment to keep.

Those elderly people who elect to spend their remaining days in their own homes in the neighborhoods where they have spent most of their lives sometimes have their wishes frustrated. The elderly are often the victims of urban renewal programs. Since they live in the older, deteriorating neighborhoods, their homes are frequently scheduled for demolition to make way for progress. In Los Angeles' Bunker Hill area, the site of a vast urban renewal project, it was largely the elderly who were displaced. Displaced older persons, because of their limited financial resources, have great difficulty finding other suitable housing. It was this problem, in part, which motivated Congress to pass in 1965 the rent subsidy bill designed to make it possible for displaced persons to find suitable housing. It is an interesting commentary on the legislative process that Congress passed the rent subsidy bill, but withheld approval of the funds necessary to implement it.

For other old people, their wish to remain in their own homes is frustrated by failing health. Though they dread the prospect, many must spend their last days in nursing homes. It is unpleasant enough for a person to have to spend his last days in an institution; the undesirable manner in which many nursing homes are operated, however, adds insult to injury. The individual should be given the opportunity to live out his life in dignity. At present, many institutionalized old people are not given this opportunity.

Most of the debates over integrated versus age-segregated "senior citizen" communities center around a concern for what is best for the older person himself. Another important point to be considered is what is best for society. If the debate is examined from this perspective, the point might well be made that it is of benefit to the community to have the elderly integrated. Their combined years represent much accumulated experience and wisdom. Undoubtedly, they can make important contributions to the welfare of their fellow citizens of all ages, if encouraged and given opportunities to do so.

Chapter 5. Employment

It is a generally accepted fact that the employment security of older workers constitutes a significant social problem. The report of the White House Conference on Aging in 1961 states:

There was general agreement that older workers in the American economy are facing acute problems relating to their employment security. The ever-increasing tempo of industrial advance and the rapidly growing complexity of technological innovations have produced a labor market in which many older workers find themselves on the margins without any secure attachment to a job, or actually displaced and unable to find employment.

There was a consensus that because employment is so important to the older person, not only for self-support and independence but also for healthful living and self-respect, basic economic and other policies should be developed in this country which will create a healthy economy and high levels of employment in all areas and for all persons in the labor market.[1]

The concept, *older worker*, is a highly relative one. There are striking and significant differences from occupation to occupation and from industry to industry in the age at which the label, *older worker*, is initially applied. For example, occupations that require great physical exertion or are deemed hazardous frequently limit employment to younger workers, whereas occupations requiring long periods of training and experience are more likely to accept older workers. The professional athlete is expected to be endowed with speed and agility. It is generally felt that by the age of 35 the average man is past his physical peak and is no longer able to compete with younger men. It is not unusual for the athlete to retire from active participation at the age of 35 or even earlier. On the other hand, the watchmaker presumably becomes more skillful as he grows older. A watchmaker seeking a position through the classified advertisements of the daily newspaper finds it to his advantage to stress that he is a mature man with 30 years of experience behind him.

In those occupations in which age limitations are applied in hiring, the

[1] Special Staff on Aging, U.S. Department of Health, Education, and Welfare, *The Nation and Its Older People: Report of the White House Conference on Aging, January 9–12, 1961* (Washington, D.C.: U.S. Government Printing Office, 1961), p. 142.

most common age boundary between the younger and the older worker is set at 45 for men. However, in some occupations (such as policeman) the maximum age for applicants may be as low as 30. One of the major airlines, in an advertisement for flight officers, set a maximum age requirement for applicants at 29 but noted that "exceptionally well qualified applicants through age 35 may be considered."[2]

For women, it is probably more common to find the maximum age for applicants to be set at 35 (or 30) than it is for men. In many women's occupations personal attractiveness (or more properly, sex appeal) is considered highly desirable or even necessary. For this reason, the acceptable age range for applicants may be very limited. Applicants for airline hostess jobs usually must be between the ages of 20 and 27. Bar maids must be over 21 and, frequently, under 30, particularly if donning an abbreviated costume and doing some dancing is part of the job. There is also a tendency to prefer young, attractive stenographic personnel to "dress up the office"; it is not unusual to set upper age limits of 30 or 35 for such jobs.

The point is that the boundary age at which a worker becomes old is relative to the particular occupation being considered and to the context in which the work is being performed. It is not possible to specify a single age after which all workers will be classified as older workers. The most prevalent boundary age, however, is probably 45.

The changing structure of the labor force

In order to understand the nature of the employment problem facing the older worker, it is necessary to examine the American labor force and the changes taking place in it.

The U.S. Bureau of the Census defines the labor force as those "persons 14 years of age or over who were employed, unemployed or in the Armed Forces during a specified week."[3] In September 1965 the total labor force was estimated at 78,044,000 workers, and its civilian component at about 75,321,000.[4] The average annual increase in the labor force is around 650,000 persons.[5] The labor force participation rate, which reflects the

[2] Los Angeles *Times*, December 19, 1965.

[3] *Statistical Abstract of the United States:* 1961 (82d ed.; Washington, D.C., 1961), p. 199.

[4] U.S. Department of Labor, *Monthly Report of the Labor Force: September 1965* (Washington, D.C., 1965), table A-1, p. 17.

[5] Gertrude Bancroft, *The American Labor Force: Its Growth and Changing Composition* (New York: John Wiley & Sons, Inc., 1958), p. 24.

proportion of the population 14 years old or older who are in the labor force, runs at about 58 per cent.

About two-thirds of those in the labor force are males and one-third, females. Approximately 78 per cent of all males aged 14 or older participate in the labor force, compared to 38 per cent of the females 14 or older.

In September 1965 the participation rate for males between the ages of 14 and 19 was 41 per cent. The rate more than doubled (to 86.9 per cent) for the 20-to-24 age group and reached a high of 97.6 per cent for men between 25 and 44. Thereafter, the rate began to decline: for men between 45 and 54 it declined to 95.3 per cent and for men between 55 and 64, to 84.3 per cent. For men 65 and over, the rate was only 28.3 per cent.[6]

The pattern of participation for women varies somewhat from the male pattern. For example, in September 1965 the rate for females between 14 and 19 was only 28.7 per cent and for those between 20 and 24, 49.6 per cent. Between the ages of 25 and 34, the rate fell to 38.6 per cent. It increased to 46.4 per cent for women between 35 and 44 and to 51.3 per cent for those between 45 and 54. Thereafter, the rate decreased to 40.6 per cent for women between 55 and 64 and plummeted to 9.7 per cent for those 65 and over.[7]

On the basis of the preceding figures, the male pattern of labor force participation is characterized by an increase from adolescence to a peak period between the ages of 25 and 44, when nearly all males are in the labor force. This peak period is followed by a gradual decline in participation up to the age of retirement. For men of retirement age the rates are considerably lower than for younger men. The pattern of female participation is characterized by an increase from adolescence through the early twenties. Thereafter, there is a decline that undoubtedly reflects the fact that many women marry, leave the labor force, at least temporarily, and begin their families. About the age of 35 (when children are ordinarily old enough to be in school) the rate begins to increase again, reaching its peak in the 45-to-54-year-old category. Beyond that category the participation rate decreases again, gradually at first, but precipitously at the age of 65.

According to the 1960 census, only 8.6 per cent of the total civilian labor force was engaged in agriculture. Among those in nonagricultural occupations, the largest proportion (almost 31 per cent) were working in manufacturing and 22 per cent in wholesale or retail trade. The third largest employment category was government, with 16 per cent of the nonagricul-

---

[6] U.S. Department of Labor, *Monthly Report of the Labor Force: September 1965*, table A-10, p. 21.

[7] *Ibid.*

tural workers.[8] The leading occupational category in 1960 was operatives and kindred workers (primarily factory workers), namely 18 per cent of the workers. The second largest category was clerical and kindred workers, 14.7 per cent. Also, in 1960, approximately 84 per cent of employed persons were wage and salary workers, only 16 per cent being self-employed or unpaid family workers.[9]

There are several long-term trends in the labor force worthy of note:[10]

1. A continuing increase in the size of the labor force. In 1900, there were approximately 27,640,000 persons in the labor force; in 1965, 78,044,000.

2. Decreasing participation rates for men in the youngest and oldest age categories. In 1900, the participation rates for males between 14 and 19 was 60.1 per cent, compared to a rate of 41 per cent in September 1965. The participation rate for males 65 years of age and over was 61.7 per cent in 1900, compared to 28.1 per cent in September 1965.

3. An increase in the participation rate of women. In 1900, 17.2 per cent of females, 14 years of age and over, were in the labor force. But in September 1965, 37.8 per cent were in the labor force.

4. A striking decrease in the proportion of the labor force engaged in agriculture. In 1900, just less than 40 per cent of the labor force was engaged in agriculture; in 1960, 8.6 per cent of the labor force was so engaged.

5. An increase in the proportion of workers in white-collar occupations. In 1900, less than 20 per cent of the workers had white-collar jobs; in September 1965, approximately 41 per cent of those in the labor force were white-collar workers.

6. A continuing shift from self-employed to wage and salary workers. In 1940, about 73 per cent of the labor force consisted of wage and salary workers; in September 1965, they accounted for approximately 84 per cent of the labor force.

7. A shift from the production of material goods to the production of services. In 1900, almost 75 per cent of those in the labor force were engaged in the production of material goods; workers producing services constituted slightly less than 25 per cent. In 1960, by contrast, 46 per cent of the workers were producing material goods, compared to 54 per cent

[8] U.S. Bureau of the Census, *Statistical Abstract of the United States: 1961*, table 268, p. 203, and table 279, p. 208 ff.

[9] *Ibid.*, table 287, p. 215.

[10] The following data are extracted from Bancroft, *The American Labor Force*: Philip M. Hauser, "Labor Force," in Robert E. L. Faris, ed., *Handbook of Modern Sociology* (Chicago: Rand McNally & Company, 1964), pp. 160–190; U.S. Bureau of the Census, *Statistical Abstract of the United States: 1961*; U.S. Department of Labor, *Monthly Report of the Labor Force: September 1965*.

who were producing services. Of the latter, 42 per cent were in white-collar occupations and 12 per cent were in household and other service occupations. Symptomatic of this shift to service occupations is the continuing increase in government workers. Between 1950 and 1960, the proportion of the civilian labor force working for government units increased from 9.6 to 12.7 per cent. Furthermore, the proportion of government workers employed by state and local governmental units increased from 68 per cent in 1950 to 73.6 per cent in 1960.

8. Although no hard statistics are available to support the contention, there is an apparent trend toward higher skill requirements. According to Hauser, "The changing occupational composition of the labor force (changes in specific ways of making a living) was the result of advancing technology making the economy less dependent than it previously was on human muscle power and much more dependent on professional, technical, and clerical skills and of modifications in the way of life which have changed consumption patterns."[11]

The changing occupational composition of which Hauser speaks increases the demand for persons with a higher level of formal education and technical training. A cursory examination of the want ads in the daily newspaper gives the impression that many jobs are available, but that, in general, qualifications for filling them include formal education, technical training, or both.

Employment patterns among older workers

Older workers constitute a significant part of the total labor force. In 1965, 37 per cent of the male workers and almost 39 per cent of the women were 45 or older.[12]

Although they are by no means a homogeneous group, it is possible to describe older workers in general terms. They tend to be much less mobile; if they have jobs, they are not likely to leave them voluntarily. After the age of 50, occupational mobility is negligible. Workers 45 years and older tend to be found in skilled, managerial, and proprietary occupations on the one hand and the low-paid, unskilled service occupations on the other. Self-employed workers are common among those in the older age categories. Members of this group tend to be farmers, small businessmen, and profes-

---

[11] *Op. cit.*, p. 184.
[12] U.S. Department of Labor, *Monthly Report of the Labor Force: September 1965*, table A-10, p. 21.

sional men.[13] About 25 per cent of the older men in the labor force are farmers or farm managers; about one-eighth are managers, officials, and proprietors.[14] Older men in these occupations can control their own destinies. They can adapt their working hours to suit their capacities and make their own decisions regarding retirement.

In manufacturing, the percentage of older workers declines progressively as their age increases and also as the company's size increases. Compulsory retirement policies, tending to force out older workers, are more common in large than in small companies. Small companies may keep older workers on even when their productive capacities decline. This practice probably reflects either the small company's inferior competitive position in the labor market or its more personalized relationship between management and workers.

Older workers are not commonly found in laboring occupations because of the heavy physical work involved. Laboring jobs are usually filled by new arrivals in the labor force; they tend to be temporary jobs through which new workers pass on their way to other occupations.

The percentage of men employed in service occupations increases sharply with age, and many men end their work lives in these occupations. About 1 of every 10 older workers is employed as a service worker:[15] he is able to get a job as a janitor, night watchman, guard, dry cleaner, and so forth. Older workers commonly find employment also in hotels, motels, rooming houses, and similar places. More than 10 per cent of the workers in the real estate business have reached or passed the age of 65.[16]

Women 45 years or over commonly hold clerical jobs, factory jobs, or jobs as professional and technical assistants. However, as their age increases the number of women in these occupations tends to decline rapidly. Women of 65 or over are often employed as household workers;[17] they may do light housework or baby-sit. For many women, these tend to be intermittent or part-time jobs to supplement retirement income.

The statement was made earlier that older workers tend to be less mobile and that occupational mobility practically disappears by the age 50.[18] This is true partly because older workers are more likely to have settled down in an occupation with which they identify and at a job they consider permanent. They may be reluctant to sacrifice seniority or rights

---

[13] B. V. H. Schneider, *The Older Worker* (Institute of Industrial Relations, University of California, Berkeley, 1962), p. 19.

[14] John J. Corson and John W. McConnell, *Economic Needs of Older People* (New York: The Twentieth Century Fund, 1956), p. 50.

[15] *Ibid.*

[16] *Ibid.*, p. 53.

[17] *Ibid.*, p. 51.

[18] See page 51 above.

to accumulated fringe benefits by changing jobs. Also, the older worker is likely to have taken on family and financial responsibilities which tie him more closely to his job. Undoubtedly, another crucial factor in the reluctance of the older worker to leave his job is the fear that he will not be able to find another one. As Morris says, "As a generalization, however, we may observe that if workers lose their jobs *for whatever reason* they are likely to have serious difficulty securing new jobs if they are forty-five or over. The amount of difficulty tends to vary according to many factors—such as sex, occupation, industry, locality, general economic conditions, and war or peace."[19]

The Bureau of the Census defines long-term unemployment as lasting 15 weeks or more. According to the labor force survey of September 1965, a larger percentage of the long-term unemployed (35 per cent) were in the 45-years-and-over category than in any other age group.[20] This is pretty convincing evidence that the older worker encounters difficulty in finding a new job once he enters the ranks of the unemployed. Furthermore, the older the unemployed worker is, the longer he is likely to remain unemployed.

Statistics that show persons aged 65 and over to have low rates of unemployment tend to be misleading, because many people in this age category become discouraged by their inability to find work and withdraw from the labor force. Unemployment is often a demoralizing experience: many men find it difficult to maintain self-respect when they are out of work. The line of least resistance for the man aged 65 or over is to declare himself retired or, at least, to deny that he is seeking work. According to the definitions used by the Bureau of the Census, a man who is not employed must be seeking work to be considered unemployed. If he is not seeking work, he is classified as being out of the labor force. Being out of the labor force is more respectable than being unemployed.

It might be expected that the older unemployed worker would compete successfully with younger job seekers. After all, the older man has the benefit of more experience behind him, and he certainly has more skill than many of the younger men, especially those entering the labor force for the first time. However, preference is given to the younger worker in a competitive labor market. The outcome of this, for the older worker, is that he must turn to jobs for which younger workers do not ordinarily compete. A common pattern in the work life cycle is for the older worker

[19] James R. Morris, *Employment Opportunities in Later Years* (Burlingame, Calif.: Foundation for Voluntary Welfare, 1960), p. 13.
[20] U.S. Department of Labor, *Monthly Report of the Labor Force: September 1965*, table A-8, p. 20.

to finish his work career in a lower paying, less prestigious occupation than he held during his prime working years.

Factors affecting participation rates of older workers

One of the definite long-term trends affecting the structure of the American labor force has been the declining participation rate of older workers. What factors are responsible for the departure of older men from the labor force?

One obvious reason for leaving the labor force is poor health. According to Corson and McConnell, about one-third of those older men who leave the labor force do so for health reasons.[21] Physical disabilities, of course, are not limited to older workers, but they are certainly more prevalent among older workers than they are among younger ones. Sawyer points out,

Invalidism increases rapidly with age. The National Health Survey showed that only one in 100 persons at ages thirty-five to forty-five was an invalid, but more than five out of 100 at ages sixty-five to seventy-four were so classified. The annual frequency of disabling illness lasting at least a week was 279 per 1,000 individuals among those sixty-five and over—almost twice the figure for those aged fifteen to sixty-four. Disabling sickness also lasts longer among the aged. The average duration of disabling disease for the elderly was 131 days per case, just twice the figure for those aged fifteen to sixty-four.[22]

This is not meant to imply that poor health is characteristic of the majority of older people. However, poor health is more common among the elderly and frequently does lead to withdrawal from the labor force.

Obsolescence of skill is another factor in the withdrawal of the older worker from the labor force. Changing technology leads to the development and expansion of some industries and the decline of others. For instance, apart from developing the automobile industry, which has become a major factor in our economy, the invention of the automobile gave a shot in the arm to the oil and rubber industries. On the other hand, the development of the automobile practically sounded the death knell for industries associated with horses: the once common livery stable is almost a thing of the past; blacksmithing is almost a lost art; the manufacture of carriages has shrunk to almost nothing.

[21] *Op. cit.,* p. 72.
[22] William A. Sawyer, "Health Considerations," in Wilma Donahue, ed., *Earning Opportunities for Older Workers* (Ann Arbor: University of Michigan Press, 1955), p. 77.

In spite of the efforts of their union, railroad firemen are gradually being displaced from jobs that have been ruled obsolete. This displacement has come about because of the conversion from steam locomotives to diesels. The courts gave the railroads the go-ahead to discharge firemen who had been on the job less than 10 years. Firemen who have worked longer than 10 years will be kept on the job until they retire, but they will not be replaced.

The continued progress of automation is bound to displace workers in the industries concerned. It has been argued that automation will benefit the working man in the long run by increasing occupational opportunities through the development of new jobs. The short-run effect of automation, however, is to displace workers from obsolete jobs. This displacement will be permanent for many older workers, because they will not be retrained for new jobs. It is considered uneconomical to retrain a man who has only a few years left in his work life; private industry, therefore, is unlikely to assume the financial burden for such retraining. If such men are to be retrained, the government will need to assume the burden, and special effort will have to be made to place them in appropriate jobs.

As was pointed out earlier, farming is a major source of employment for the older worker. However, mechanization of farming has led to a drastic reduction of the farm-labor force. Many of the industries in which large numbers of older workers are found are, in fact, declining industries. The developing and expanding industries are those for which the older workers seldom have the requisite skills and training. The newer industries characteristically employ the younger, more highly skilled workers.

Adding to the difficulties of the older worker is the fact that he generally has had less education than his younger competitor. Both job opportunities and opportunities for advancement are often dependent upon the candidate's level of formal education. The older worker is barred from consideration for many jobs because he cannot meet the minimal educational requirements. The decrease in the labor force participation rate of older men is almost evenly matched by the increasing participation rate of women. It may be hypothesized that in some jobs the older men are being replaced by women with more education and training.

Plant relocation is sometimes responsible for removing older workers from the labor force. Industrial concerns seek locations with inexpensive land, cheap labor, and favorable tax structures. It is not unusual for a company to move a plant from a high-wage to a low-wage area. For example, there has been an almost complete migration of textile plants from New England to the Southern states. When a company abandons a location, many workers are left behind. Older workers are less likely than the younger ones to follow the plant to its new location. Instead of moving, some older workers will withdraw from the labor force.

Compulsory retirement policies are an increasingly important factor in removing older workers from the labor force. There is a growing tendency, especially among larger companies, to make retirement at the age of 65 mandatory. Pension plans are becoming more common in private industry; such plans are generally accompanied by involuntary retirement provisions. Workers subject to compulsory retirement are still in the minority; among those covered by pension plans, however, the proportion subject to compulsory retirement is high.

Finally, there are those who look forward with anticipation to retirement and make plans for their retirement years. When they reach retirement age, they leave the labor force not because of ill health nor because they are forced to, but because they want to retire.

According to the governmental labor force survey of September 1965, approximately 3,124,000 persons aged 65 and over were still in the labor force.[23] What are the factors that explain the continued participation of these people after they have reached the normal retirement age?

Probably the major reason for continued participation in the labor force is financial. The U.S. Bureau of the Census estimated that in 1962, almost 90 per cent of unrelated individuals in the 65-and-over age category had annual incomes of less than $3,000. Furthermore, it was estimated that the average income of families headed by persons aged 65 or over was 46 per cent below the national average.[24] Though more than 200,000 older Americans had annual incomes of $20,000 or more in 1961, they constituted just a little more than 1 per cent of the 65-and-over age category.[25] The median family income for two-person families in which the head of the family was 65 or over was $2,530 in 1960.[26] This means that 50 per cent of these families were living on incomes of less than $2,530 a year. The median income for persons 65 and over living alone in 1960 was $1,055.[27] From these figures it is evident that the affluent senior citizen is the exception rather than the rule.

About 45 per cent of wage and salary workers in private industry are

[23] U.S. Department of Labor, *Monthly Report of the Labor Force: September 1965*, table A-10, p. 21.

[24] "Income of Families and Persons in the United States: 1962," *Current Population Reports: Consumer Income*, Series P-60, No. 41, October 21, 1963 (Washington, D.C.: U.S. Government Printing Office), p. 13.

[25] President's Council on Aging, *The Older American* (Washington, D.C.: U.S. Government Printing Office, 1963), p. 7.

[26] *Ibid.*, p. 9.

[27] *Ibid.*, p. 10.

covered by private pension plans. However, these plans typically provide benefits amounting to between 20 to 40 per cent of preretirement incomes for long-term employees; the benefits are even less for workers with shorter periods of service.[28] For many of the aged, a pension provides for less than a minimum-subsistence income. Nor does Social Security guarantee economic security. As of 1963, approximately 75 per cent of persons aged 65 and over were eligible for Social Security benefits.[29] The maximum benefits under Social Security have been gradually increasing, but they are hardly sufficient to provide a comfortable living. In 1965, the maximum monthly benefit was $135.90, based on an average preretirement monthly wage of $400; the minimum was $44. The maximum monthly benefit a husband and wife, both aged 65 or over, could collect was $203.70.

The U.S. Bureau of Labor Statistics has estimated a "modest but adequate" budget for a couple 65 and older who rent a small house or apartment. The estimate is based upon the kinds and amounts of goods and services deemed necessary to maintain an adequate level of living. The prices used in the budget estimate were based on current prices (1959) in 20 cities—most of them large. The annual minimum income arrived at by the Bureau was $3,010.[30] Obviously, a couple collecting the maximum benefits under Social Security—and very few of them do collect the maximum amount—would fall short of this "modest but adequate" budget. The couple's annual income would be $2,444.40—an income falling below the Bureau's figure by more than $500.

Persons not covered by some pension plan or by Social Security (and few workers make adequate provisions on their own for retirement) have no choice but to continue working or else to apply for old-age assistance. Those covered by pension plans or Social Security frequently must work, at least part time, to supplement their meager incomes. Governmental employees and others covered by pension plans but not by Social Security frequently work after retirement at different jobs, in order to qualify for Social Security benefits.

In times of labor shortages there is societal pressure to keep older workers in the labor force and bring retired workers back in. During World War II there was a temporary reversal of the long-term trend toward decreasing labor force participation of older men; in 1940, the participation rate for men 65 and over was 42.2. The rate began to climb with the outbreak of the war, reaching 49.5 per cent in 1943, 50.9 per cent in 1944,

[28] *Ibid.*, p. 11.
[29] *Ibid.*
[30] *Ibid.*, p. 10.

and 50.8 per cent in 1945. Thereafter, the rate returned to its long-term pattern of decreasing participation.[31]

For some older workers, factors associated with their jobs may be responsible for keeping them in the labor force. Men who sincerely enjoy their work are reluctant to retire, and self-employed professional and business men frequently have no intentions of retiring. But men whose jobs are inherently uninteresting are most likely to want to retire.[32] Other men continue to work, not because the particular job they hold is important to them, but because it is important to them to be working. They feel that work is the source of their self-respect, and they cannot bear to be without a job of some kind. For others, it is the opportunity to associate with fellow workers that is important; they resist retirement because they fear the resulting isolation. Still others associate retirement with declining physical and mental capacities and impending death and cling to work as a form of denial of the inevitable.

Discrimination against older workers

Many older workers desperately hold on to jobs they do not really like because they fear that if they lose them they will not be able to find others. These fears are not unfounded: there is no question that older workers are confronted by very real barriers to reemployment.

In 1960, Morris conducted a survey of the hiring practices of large private employers[33]; he sent questionnaires to 300 of the largest firms in the United States. These firms included 200 industrial corporations, 20 large commercial banking firms, 20 merchandising firms, 20 transportation companies, 20 life insurance firms, and 20 utility companies. Of these questionnaires, 51 per cent were either fully or partially filled out and returned. Morris found that 14 per cent of the responding firms did not generally hire hourly male workers beyond the age of 45 or some other lower age; 22 per cent applied these age limits to male salaried workers. The comparable figures for female workers were 21 per cent for hourly workers and 25 per cent for salaried workers. The crucial age barrier appeared to be the age of 50. Of the responding firms, 37 per cent did not hire hourly male workers beyond the age of 50, and 40 per cent did not hire male salaried workers beyond this age. The comparable figures for females were 36 per cent for hourly workers and 41 per cent for salaried workers. Specific age restrictions

[31] U.S. Bureau of the Census, *Historical Statistics of the United States, Colonial Times to 1957* (Washington, D.C.: U.S. Government Printing Office, 1960), Series D 13–25, p. 71.

[32] See Chapter 6.

[33] *Op. cit.*, p. 29 ff.

were more commonly imposed on female than on male workers and on salaried workers than on hourly workers. Utility companies appeared to be least likely to hire older workers. Interestingly enough, Morris found that only 6 per cent of the firms responding attempted to study the relevance of age at the time of hiring to subsequent performance on the job.

A large-scale study of age barriers to hiring was conducted in 1956 by the U.S. Bureau of Employment Security in seven large labor market areas: Detroit, Michigan; Los Angeles, California; Miami, Florida; Minneapolis–St. Paul, Minnesota; Philadelphia, Pennsylvania; Seattle, Washington; and Worcester, Massachusetts.[34] It was found that maximum age limits were specified in job orders filed with public employment offices 58 per cent of the time. The age limit was set at under 35 in 20 per cent of the cases, under 45 in 41 per cent of the cases, and under 55 in 52 per cent of the cases. The proportion of job orders specifying various maximum ages (all under age 55) varied from 28 per cent for skilled jobs to 68 per cent for clerical jobs. The various occupational groups could be arranged in rank order from most likely to least likely to set age limits as follows: clerical, unskilled, professional and managerial, sales, service, semiskilled, and skilled.

It was also possible to rank industries according to the frequency with which age limits were specified in job orders. This ranking from most likely to least likely to specify was as follows: (1) finance, insurance, and real estate; (2) transportation, communication, and utilities; (3) wholesale and retail trade; (4) durable-goods manufacturing; (5) nondurable-goods manufacturing; (6) government; (7) construction; and (8) service.

Size of firm was also found to be a significant variable in imposing age restrictions in hiring. In firms with seven or fewer employees, age restrictions were specified in 52 per cent of the cases. In firms with 1,000 or more employees, such restrictions were specified in 78 per cent of the cases.

How do employers justify discrimination in the hiring of workers based upon age? In the U.S. Bureau of Employment Security study, nine reasons were given for imposing age restrictions in hiring.[35] The reasons given, in rank order according to frequency of mention, were as follows:

1. Older workers are not as efficient as younger workers. They are not able to maintain the production standards set by the company.

2. Older workers cannot meet the physical requirements set by the company. They lack the strength, stamina, and endurance necessary to do the work.

---

[34] The study is reported in Governor's Commission on the Employment and Retirement Problems of Older Workers, *Employment and Retirement of Older Workers* (Sacramento, Calif.: California State Printing Office, 1960), p. 31 ff.

[35] *Ibid.*, p. 33.

3. Older workers are set in their ways. They are unable to make the necessary adjustments to a new work situation. It is not possible to orient them to company policies and practices.

4. It is not economically feasible to hire the older workers, because their presence would lead to increased pension and insurance costs.

5. The older workers are above or too close to the compulsory retirement age established by the company. They would not qualify for a pension, and the company frowns upon hiring workers who are not pensionable.

6. The company policy is to hire younger workers, and there is reluctance to mix different age groups.

7. Older workers are too difficult to train for new jobs; they do not catch on fast enough. It is more expensive to train older workers, and the short time they have left to work after being trained makes training economically unsound.

8. Older workers tend to be ill more often than younger workers and miss too much work.

9. The policy is to promote from within the company. Older workers do not fit in with this policy. It would be a violation of policy to hire them on some higher level, yet it would be unfair to them to hire them at the lower levels.

Employers are not solely responsible for age discrimination in hiring. Though many union policies are designed to protect the interests of the older worker, the policies of some unions actually foster discriminatory hiring practices based on age. As Morris points out, seniority provisions and apprenticeship programs may act as barriers to the employment of older workers.[36] Seniority provisions serve to protect the jobs of older workers who are employed, but they tend to minimize employment opportunities for older "outsiders." The practice is to make seniority a major criterion for advancement within a company. Older unemployed workers who are skilled and experienced presumably could qualify for middle-range jobs. The seniority principle, however, operates to the advantage of those already employed. The union generally balks at management's attempts to put new workers into the hierarchy anywhere but at the bottom. Bottom-rung positions, on the other hand, usually are filled by new arrivals in the labor force. Apprenticeship programs discriminate against older workers because they frequently specify maximum age limits for entry. In the unions' view, apprenticeship programs aim at training young workers—not at retraining older ones.

When jobs are scarce, unions push for early retirement of older workers

[36] *Op. cit.*, p. 64 ff.

to make room for younger ones. Therefore, unions stress improved retirement benefits, either through private pension plans or through extension of the Social Security program.

The abilities of older workers

To what extent are the basic nine common reasons for not hiring older workers, which imply that this group is less productive, supported by the facts?

First, older workers are not a homogeneous group: productivity at the age of 45 and over is as variable as in younger workers. Second, the demands of different jobs defy generalization. Although the ability to do heavy labor does decline with age, this decline is gradual. In physically less demanding jobs, older workers often perform as well as or better than younger ones.

For example, the U.S. Bureau of Labor Statistics, in a comparative productivity study of 6,000 office workers in different age categories,[37] found that the productivity of older workers was comparable to that of younger ones, and that the older workers had a steadier weekly rate of output. A series of studies by the Nuffield Unit for Research into Problems of Aging in Great Britain found that performance declines from the twenties on, but that, significantly, there were increasing differences in the performances of people in the same age categories as they grew older.[38] Thus, many older people are still capable of doing heavy work and many do such work.

Significant also is the Bureau of Labor Statistics' finding that workers aged 45 and over have better safety records than do younger ones,[39] the highest rate of disabling injuries on the job being in the 35–44 age category and the highest rate of nondisabling injuries, in the 25–29 group. The rates decreased steadily with increasing age, reaching the lowest point in the 70–74 age category. Older workers also have better absenteeism records than younger ones, largely because of a selective factor. As older workers in poor health tend to drop out of the labor force, those who continue to work are the healthier ones.

There is some truth to the belief that older workers tend to be more set in their ways and, hence, less adaptable. It must be stressed again, however, that older persons do not form a homogeneous group; there is much variability among them. Many older persons *are* adaptable and have dem-

[37] Schneider, *op. cit.*, p. 45.
[38] *Ibid.*, p. 40.
[39] *Ibid.*, p. 37.

onstrated this by successfully making significant changes in occupations late in life. Also, the older worker's greater experience often helps him in approaching new problems. The question is not whether it is possible to teach an old dog new tricks, but whether the required investment is economically sound.

It is also true that having large numbers of older workers in one's employ may increase pension and insurance costs. However, many more older workers than currently are could be absorbed by large industries without substantially increasing costs. Furthermore, Morris has suggested that employers who have pension plans might hire older workers with the understanding that they would not come under pension coverage.[40] Working without pension coverage is preferable to not working at all.

In weighing the pro's and con's of hiring older workers, it can be said that the advantages and disadvantages practically cancel each other. Much of the prejudice against older workers is based upon myth and misinformation. These myths must be exploded through effective education programs. Then, perhaps, employers (and unions) will accept older workers, not as a special category of labor, but as individuals and on their individual merits.

[40] *Op. cit.*, p. 55.

Chapter 6. Retirement

To a significant extent the American value system is a product of our Puritan heritage. The virtues of hard work were widely extolled by our Puritan forefathers; lack of industry was considered to be a grievous sin. As Wright says,

If the Protestants, especially the Puritan elements of Protestantism, did not invent the gospel of work, they adopted it with such enthusiasm that it became a cardinal point in their social doctrine. One reason for the Puritans' insistence upon education was the fear that ignorance would beget idleness, and idleness, which was the waste of God's precious time—a recurring phrase in Puritan writing—was one of the worst of sins. The Puritans were convinced that education increased piety and "piety bred industry," a desirable end in itself. Judge Samuel Sewall, mindful of the waste of time on April Fools' Day, wrote to Ezekiel Cheever the schoolmaster on April 1, 1708, complaining about the foolish doings: "If men are accountable for every idle word, what a reckoning will they have that keep up stated times to promote lying and folly," he fumes. "What an abuse is it of precious time; what a profanation! What an affront of the devine bestower of it." Sewall hoped that Cheever would warn his pupils against idleness and idle pleasures. Thomas Shepard, writing to his son at Harvard in 1672, warned him against wasting time: "Abhor therefore one hour of idleness as you would be ashamed of one hour of drunkenness." Cotton Mather in numerous passages expounds the gospel of work and inveighs against the iniquity of idleness. When he looked about Boston at the turn of the century, he saw relaxation of the early strenuousness that saddened him. "Idleness, alas!" he sighed, "idleness increases in the town exceedingly; idleness of which there never came any goodness! idleness which is the 'reproach of any people.'" To Mather's distress, beggars had been seen on the streets of Boston, beggars whom "our Lord Jesus Christ himself hath expressly forbidden us to countenance." If they refuse to work, the poor must not eat, Mather believed, for refusal to work was a sin against God himself.[1]

Though work no longer has the predominantly religious overtones it once had, our Puritan heritage has had a lasting influence in endowing work with positive value. There is a general feeling that an adult male, to

[1] Louis B. Wright, *The Cultural Life of the American Colonies: 1607–1763* (New York: Harper Torchbooks, Harper & Row, Publishers, Inc., 1962), p. 25.

be a respected member of the community, must hold a steady job. In fact, holding a steady job is a prerequisite for achieving adult status in our society. The college student, even though he has attained the age of 21, is not fully accepted in the adult community until he secures a full-time job. In our society, securing the first full-time job almost constitutes a rite of passage equivalent to the puberty rites practiced in other societies.

The single most important source of recognition for the American male is his job. In earlier days, when a stranger was encountered he was asked his family name and place of residence; an attempt was made to identify him in terms of his family ties. If he was found to be one of the Smiths from Hartford, for example, he ceased to be a stranger.

Today when we meet a stranger, we are more likely to ask him what he does for a living. With our vast population, seeking to fit him into a niche through his family name is usually fruitless. However, finding out what kind of work he does provides us with an occupational stereotype that guides our behavior toward him. We are given a clue not only to what behavior is appropriate for us, but also to what behavior to expect from him.

Work experiences are not generally central to the lives of women. Although more and more women work, they are not under societal pressure to do so. Women achieve status through their husbands. It is not unusual to inquire of the married female stranger, "What does your husband do for a living?" The husband's occupation usually determines his nuclear family's place in the social structure.

Because work is so important to the man, we begin at an early stage of life to prepare the male child for a productive adulthood. Little boys are encouraged to play at various occupations. At first, their choices are not very practical: few of them will ever become cowboys, or detectives or astronauts. The important thing is that they begin to think about filling some occupational role when they grow up. They soon learn that work is an integral part of the life of the adult male. At an early stage parents and other adults begin to instill in the child the attitudes and values related to work. He is taught that he should be industrious and ambitious; he is soundly criticized for being lazy.

Boys are encouraged to develop masculine interests associated with work and occupations. Trucks and tools are favored toys for little boys. Dolls are taboo! When a boy reaches his early teens, he is encouraged to get a paper route, to cut grass, or to shovel snow. Mother may even frame the first dollar her son earns. Before too long, the positive value of work is deeply ingrained in the personality of the growing boy.

Throughout his productive years the man is judged in terms of his work experiences. His primary source of prestige is his occupation. The commitment to work is frequently even more basic than the commitment to a particular occupation. The first requirement for respectability is that a man work. Beyond that, differential prestige is bestowed on him according to his occupation.

Nancy S. Morse and Robert S. Weiss asked a random sample of employed men if they would quit or continue to work if they inherited enough money to live comfortably without working.[2] Of the men queried, 80 per cent said they would continue to work. There was also an age differential in the percentages of men who would continue to work. Between the ages of 21 and 34, 90 per cent would continue to work; between 35 and 44, 83 per cent; between 45 and 54, 72 per cent; between 55 and 64, 61 per cent; and of those 65 and over, 82 per cent. It seems that as a man grows older, he resigns himself to the fact that he will eventually have to retire. The percentage who would continue to work is high for those 65 and over; however, these respondents are not representative of all men in this age category. Rather, they represent employed men in this age group. A large percentage of these men probably elected to remain in the labor force even though they were of retirement age.

A second question asked the subjects why they would, or would not, continue to work. Of those who would continue, 63 per cent gave reasons Morse and Weiss classified as positive: "enjoy the kind of work," 9 per cent; "to be associated with people," 1 per cent; "to keep occupied (interested)," 32 per cent; "justifies my existence," 5 per cent; "gives feeling of self-respect," 5 per cent; "keeps individually healthy, good for a person," 10 per cent; and other reasons, 1 per cent.[3] Of the respondents who would continue, 37 per cent gave reasons classified as negative: "would feel lost, go crazy," 14 per cent; "would feel useless," 2 per cent; "would feel bored," 4 per cent; "would not know what to do with my time, can't be idle," 10 per cent; "habit, inertia," 6 per cent; and "to keep out of trouble," 1 per cent.[4] It should be noted, in passing, that what Morse and Weiss classify as "negative" or "positive" responses are, to a considerable degree, interchangeable. Thus, "to keep occupied" might just as well have been classified as a negative rather than a positive response, and "would feel bored" might just as well have been classified as a positive rather than a negative response.

Significantly, only 9 per cent of those who would continue to work said they would do so because they enjoyed their kind of work. This finding supports the statement that to be working is more important than one's

[2] "The Function and Meaning of Work and the Job," *American Sociological Review*, XX (1955), p. 198.
[3] *Ibid.*, p. 192.
[4] *Ibid.*

particular occupation. The kinds of reasons offered for wanting to continue working reflect a dominant belief that work is a necessary part of man's existence.

Morse and Weiss conclude:

The results indicate that for most men working does not simply function as a means of earning a livelihood. Even if there were no economic necessity for them to work, most men would work anyway. It is through the producing role that most men tie into society, and for this reason and others, most men find the producing role important for maintaining their sense of well-being.[5]

The evidence clearly warrants the conclusion that work is central to the life of the average American male, a fact he is repeatedly reminded of. And increasingly, work is becoming a central life interest for many American women.

The dilemma of retirement

The increase in life expectancy and the accompanying increase in the number of persons aged 65 and over make retirement an ever more common phenomenon in our society. There is a definite long-term trend toward a decreasing rate of participation in the labor force among older men. Although, psychologically, it might make sense to raise the retirement age in view of the increasing number of men living past 65, there are, in fact, economic and sociological pressures to hold the retirement age at 65, or even to lower it. There is concern that employment opportunities are not expanding fast enough to accommodate both the young men seeking to enter the labor force and the old men seeking to remain in it. Emphasis on higher levels of education helps, somewhat, to delay the entry of young men into the labor force. Compulsory retirement policies and a Social Security option that allows a man to retire at 62 with a reduced rate of compensation are designed to get the older man to leave the labor force and make room for others.

Changes in the distribution of occupational opportunities tend to force older men out of the labor force. For example, older men have a higher participation rate in agricultural than in nonagricultural occupations; by 1961, however, the percentage of the labor force engaged in agricultural occupations was down to just a little more than 8 per cent.[6] Also, with the

[5] *Ibid.*, p. 198.
[6] U.S. Bureau of the Census, *Statistical Abstract of the United States: 1961* (82d ed.; Washington, D.C., 1961), table 268, p. 203.

advent of automation, many of the jobs held by older men are becoming obsolete. The jobs being created through automation are largely those requiring both a higher level of skill and different kinds of skills than older workers have.

Fred Slavick and Seymour L. Wolfbein report that the labor force participation rate among men 65 and over decreased from 68.3 per cent in 1900 to 35.6 per cent in 1958.[7] The decrease in participation rate has been consistent except for the World War II period, when an acute labor shortage drew many older men and women back into the labor force. This decrease in labor force participation rates reflects the current widely held expectation that the worker will retire at the age of 65.

Tibbitts says:

Retirement is a relatively new phenomenon in our society and the challenge of a new way of life for most Americans. In rural, preindustrial days there were comparatively few older adults, and most of them were occupied with the responsibilities of making a living until overtaken by final illness or death. Until well into the last quarter of the nineteenth century, the population 65 years of age and older numbered fewer than two million—less than 3.5 per cent of the total. The population 50 years and over accounted for less than 12 per cent of the whole. Well over two-thirds lived in rural areas, and three-quarters of the older men were gainfully employed. The older women were also usefully occupied, for in the days of the self-sufficient, productive family unit they were busy cooking, sewing, cleaning, teaching and entertaining the young, and caring for the sick.

Partial or complete retirement from these tasks is a development, primarily, of the last fifty to seventy-five years. Fundamentally, it is an outgrowth of the scientific and technological achievements of the time.[8]

The dilemma retirement presents for the American man arises from the fact that the leisurely life expected of the retired contradicts the pervasive work orientation of our society. The man who has spent 40 years or more in the labor force, devoting a major portion of his life to his job, is suddenly handed a gold watch in recognition of his faithful service and told to go home and relax. For many men this is a difficult adjustment to make. The man who has devoted his life to work frequently has nothing to substitute for it once it is denied him, for relaxation is to him an art unknown.

The gist of the retirement problem is that, at least for the time being,

---

[7] "The Evolving Work-Life Pattern," in Clark Tibbitts, ed., *Handbook of Social Gerontology* (Chicago: University of Chicago Press, 1960), p. 301.

[8] Clark Tibbitts, "Retirement Problems in American Society," *The American Journal of Sociology*, LIX, No. 4 (1954), p. 301. © 1954 by The University of Chicago and Published by the University of Chicago Press.

our society does not yet accord to retirement the positive value it accords to work. Instead, there is a tendency to look on retirement as a bench mark signifying declining physical and mental prowess and impending death.

A second related problem arises from the fact that retirement has not yet become institutionalized. According to Thompson,

> In an important sense, retirement is what one makes of it. Unlike most changes in status, a correlative institutionalized role does not typically await the retiree. Instead, he must create for himself a pattern of activities which serves as an effective substitute for his job. Thus adjustment in retirement involves a considerable personal input, over and above that required to assimilate new activities and patterns of interaction which stand ready-made and waiting as part of a well-defined institutional structure.[9]

It is probable that institutionalization of retirement will be accompanied by a positive value orientation, which will facilitate the transition from work to retirement. Until such institutionalization is accomplished and until such a positive value orientation evolves, retirement will continue to pose psychological and social problems.

The concept of adjustment

The searching question being asked about retired people is "What kind of adjustment have they made?" It is a difficult question to answer. Part of the difficulty arises out of the ambiguity of the concept of adjustment. In studying adjustment of older people, researchers have taken diverse but related approaches to the measurement of adjustment. No attempt will be made to catalogue the measures used in the many studies that have appeared. However, a few of the different measures will be reviewed here to indicate the kinds of approaches taken.

Taves and Hansen sought to measure the *personal adjustment* of 6,700 persons over 65. The measurement scales they used consisted of items covering six areas: health, family, work, friendship, religion and morale. They say:

> Good personal adjustment as measured by this scale involves feeling good about one's health, enjoying a number of close friendships, satisfaction with work, finding security or comfort in religion, feeling useful, placing positive value on the later years, being relatively happy (i.e., relative to one's earlier

[9] Wayne E. Thompson, "Pre-Retirement Anticipation and Adjustment in Retirement," *The Journal of Social Issues*, XIV (1958), p. 35.

life), and experiencing satisfaction with one's family, excluding domination from and rejection by the family.[10]

In a study of 1,211 persons 60 years of age or older, Gordon F. Streib looked for factors related to high morale.[11] He used three scales designed to measure what he identified as the three major components of morale; goal centeredness, satisfaction with present life situation, and reaction to danger or adversity.[12] By goal centeredness, Streib meant the tendency to plan ahead for one's future. Satisfaction with present life situation is self-explanatory. Reaction to danger and adversity was measured by having the interviewer rate the subject's "hardships."

In a later study, Thompson, Streib, and Kosa used three indices to measure personal adjustment.[13] These indices were: satisfaction with life, dejection, and hopelessness. The researchers found an ordered relationship between their three indices. They found that the person who had a feeling of hopelessness was also likely to be dejected and dissatisfied with life. The person who did not feel hopeless but did feel dejected was also likely to be dissatisfied. But the person who was satisfied was unlikely to be either dejected or to feel hopeless. The most extreme form of personal maladjustment was marked by a feeling of hopelessness.

The common theme that runs through these and most other attempts to measure adjustment is a concern with the individual's feeling of well-being and self-fulfillment. The emphasis is on the individual's evaluation of himself and his present circumstances.

Another, more sociological conception of adjustment also is relevant. This is the evaluation others make of an individual's adjustment. The individual may be very happy with himself and his circumstances, but society may consider him maladjusted. Persons who appear to be perfectly happy are sometimes branded as eccentrics by society because their behavior is not strictly conventional.

Since social problems are defined as such by society, it is obvious that adjustment must be looked at in sociological as well as individual terms. As far as society is concerned, it is not enough for an individual to be content; in addition, his behavior must be reasonably conventional. Successful adjustment, then, means that the individual must find self-fulfillment

[10] Marvin J. Taves and Gary D. Hansen, "Exploration in Personal Adjustment after Age 65," paper read at the annual meetings of the American Sociological Association, St. Louis, Mo., August, 1961, p. 2.

[11] "Morale of the Retired," *Social Problems*, III (1956), pp. 270–276.

[12] *Ibid.*

[13] Wayne E. Thompson, Gordon F. Streib, and John Kosa, "The Effect of Retirement on Personal Adjustment: A Panel Analysis," *Journal of Gerontology*, XV (1960), pp. 165–169.

through socially acceptable means. Perhaps one of the reasons why adjustment to retirement is a problem is that society has not defined clearly those socially acceptable means whereby the retired person may find self-fulfillment. Again, this points to the need to institutionalize the retired status.

Factors related to successful adjustment

Keeping in mind the ways in which the concept of adjustment has been defined and measured, let us examine some of the variables that have rather consistently been found to be related to successful adjustment.

Contrary to popular belief, making a successful adjustment to retirement is not a universal problem. Many people are able to retire gracefully and adjust to the change almost immediately. In late 1965 Louis Harris, in a national survey, asked retired people, "Has retirement fulfilled your expectations for a good life or have you found it less than satisfactory?"[14] Of the respondents, 61 per cent said that retirement had fulfilled their expectations; 33 per cent found retirement less than satisfactory; and 6 per cent were not sure whether or not retirement had fulfilled their expectations. Among the reasons the dissatisfied gave for their plight were financial problems, 40 per cent; health poor or disabled, 28 per cent; miss working, 22 per cent; and spouse passed away, 10 per cent.[15] Although a majority of retired people eventually make successful adjustments, the fact that as many as one-third of them are not satisfied qualifies adjustment as a significant social problem.

But what factors distinguish those who make a successful adjustment from those who do not? In his national study of persons 60 years of age and over, Streib pinpointed at least three of the relevant variables.[16] The three variables he considered to be major determinants of level of morale are work status, socioeconomic status, and health.

Slightly more than half (51 per cent) of the people in Streib's sample were retired. Streib found significant differences in the morale levels of those who were retired and those who still were employed. Among the employed, 38 per cent scored low on morale; among the retired, 62 per cent.[17]

Socioeconomic status affected morale to about the same extent as retirement. Among those with high socioeconomic status, 38 per cent had low

---

[14] Los Angeles *Times*, November 29, 1965.
[15] *Ibid.*
[16] "Morale of the Retired," p. 271.
[17] *Ibid.*, p. 272.

morale, compared to 60 per cent of those with low socioeconomic status. Socioeconomic status also had a significant effect on the morale of the retired. Whereas 69 per cent of the retired with low socioeconomic status scored low on morale, only 49 per cent of those with high socioeconomic status did so.[18]

Health also had an important bearing upon the kind of adjustment made. Streib found that two-thirds of the people studied were in "good" health and one-third in "poor" health. Of those in good health, 43 per cent scored low on morale; of those in poor health, 67 per cent. Among the retired, 55 per cent of those in good health scored low on morale, compared to 71 per cent of those in poor health.[19]

When work status, socioeconomic status, and health were analyzed simultaneously to determine their combined effect upon morale, the smallest proportion of individuals with high morale (29 per cent) was found among those who were retired and in poor health. For this particular group, it did not seem to matter whether their socioeconomic status was high or low. The largest proportion of high morale (75 per cent) was found among those still employed, in good health, and with high socioeconomic status.

Streib's findings jibe with the findings of the Harris Survey. Harris found that the three most frequently mentioned reasons for finding retirement unsatisfactory were financial problems, poor health, and "miss working."[20] The Taves and Hansen study, alluded to previously, presents similar findings.[21] Hence the evidence is pretty convincing that work status, socioeconomic status, and health are key variables in the successful adjustment of elderly people.

Circumstances of retirement

An increasingly common phenomenon in private industry and government is compulsory retirement. In most cases, the mandatory retirement age is 65. In some government positions, however, the retirement age is as low as 55 or even 50, the common retirement ages for policemen and firemen. Among military men, except in unusual circumstances, mandatory retirement comes at the end of 20 years of service, regardless of age. The practice of compulsory retirement raises an important question about the

[18] *Ibid.*, p. 273.
[19] *Ibid.*, p. 274.
[20] See page 70 above.
[21] *Op. cit.*

effects of such policies on the subsequent adjustment of those retired. Do persons who retire voluntarily normally make better adjustments than persons who are forced to retire?

The study by Thompson, Streib, and Kosa sought an answer to this question.[22] The researchers compared the adjustment scores of voluntary retirees with those of compulsory retirees. They found the factor crucial to subsequent adjustment was not whether the company or the individual decided upon his retirement, but whether the individual had a favorable or unfavorable preretirement attitude toward retirement. Those who had unfavorable preretirement attitudes but retired voluntarily were more likely to become dissatisfied in retirement than those who had favorable preretirement attitudes but were forced to retire. Among the former, 64 per cent of those who had been satisfied with life prior to retirement became dissatisfied after retirement. Among the latter, 39 per cent of those who had been satisfied with life before retirement became dissatisfied after retirement. Interestingly enough, among those with favorable preretirement attitudes who were forced to retire, 42 per cent of those dissatisfied with life before retirement became satisfied after retirement. Among those with unfavorable preretirement attitudes who retired voluntarily, only 26 per cent of those who had been dissatisfied with life prior to retirement became satisfied after retirement.[23]

As an adjunct to the compulsory retirement plans, many firms have instituted preretirement planning and counseling programs. The philosophy is that adequate planning and counseling before retirement will lead to successful adjustment to retirement. Thompson's study provides interesting data on preretirement planning and counseling programs.[24] He related differences in adjustment to retirement to differences in anticipation before retirement. The three anticipatory factors he studied were preconception of retirement, preretirement attitude toward retirement, and having plans for retirement. The indices he used to measure adjustment to retirement were (1) length of time required to get used to retirement, (2) difficulty in keeping busy, and (3) dissatisfaction with retirement.

Thompson found that all three anticipatory factors were related to successful adjustment. Furthermore, the three anticipatory factors themselves were interrelated. Thus, a person who plans for retirement is likely to have an accurate preconception of retirement and a favorable attitude toward retirement.

Yet, Thompson found that planning for retirement was relatively unim-

[22] Thompson, Streib, and Kosa, *op. cit.*
[23] *Ibid.*, table 2, p. 168.
[24] "Pre-Retirement Anticipation and Adjustment to Retirement."

portant for successful adjustment compared to having an accurate preconception of retirement and a favorable preretirement attitude. Planning seemed to be important only when the individual had a favorable preretirement attitude and an accurate preconception. If the opposite was true, planning did not increase his chances of making a successful adjustment.[25]

The Thompson findings by no means nullify the importance of preretirement counseling programs. One may ask, however, whether such programs can effectively develop favorable attitudes toward and accurate preconceptions of retirement. It seems necessary to make development of favorable attitudes and accurate preconceptions an integral part of preretirement counseling programs.

The meaning of work related to retirement

Another variable that must be given serious consideration in any discussion of adjustment to retirement is the meaning work, *per se*, has for the individual. Friedmann and Havighurst and their colleagues conducted a series of studies in which they compared the meanings work had for their subjects with subjects' attitudes toward retirement.[26] Five kinds of workers were studied: steel workers, coal miners, skilled craftsmen in the printing trades, department store sales persons, and older physicians. The studies were guided by four hypotheses:

1. Work has recognized meanings in addition to that of earning a living.
2. Those persons who regard work as primarily a way of earning a living will prefer to retire at age 65 (or normal retirement age).
3. Those persons who stress values of work other than that of earning a living will prefer to continue working past 65.
4. The extra-economic meanings of work are stressed to a greater extent by members of the higher skilled occupational groups.[27]

According to Friedmann and Havighurst, work serves five distinct functions: 1. It provides the individual with income or economic return. 2. It regulates the person's pattern of life activity. 3. It bestows status on the person within his group. 4. It fixes his patterns of association with other people. 5. It offers the worker a meaningful set of life experiences.[28]

[25] *Ibid.*, p. 43.
[26] Eugene A. Friedmann and Robert J. Havighurst, *The Meaning of Work and Retirement* (Chicago: The University of Chicago Press, 1954).
[27] *Ibid.*, p. 7.
[28] *Ibid.*, p. 4.

Although their data were not strictly comparable for all five studies, they were able to make the following comparisons:

1. The workers of lower skill and socioeconomic status are more likely to see their work as having no other meaning than that of earning money.

2. The five occupational groups all value "association" about equally as a meaning of work.

3. Work as a routine which makes the time pass is recognized about equally by all five groups.

4. All groups discover self-respect and secure respect or recognition from others by means of their work, and there is probably no reliable difference among them in the prevalence of this meaning. While it seems to be highest among the skilled craftsmen, this may have resulted from the fact that the category, "Service to others," was not used in that particular study, and anyone to whom this meaning was especially significant may have mentioned self-respect or the respect of others which he obtained as a result of the service element in his work.

5. The physicians show a high awareness of the "Service to others" meaning in their work. This may be characteristic of the "service" professions.

6. Work is important as a source of interesting, purposeful activity and a source of intrinsic enjoyment for all five groups, but there may be reliable differences between them in this respect.[29]

In general, the findings of the five studies supported the hypotheses relating meaning of work to attitudes toward retirement. There was evidence that those who attached extra-economic meanings to work were those who were most reluctant to retire, whereas those who looked upon work merely as a means of earning a living tended to look forward to retirement. Extra-economic meanings of work were most common among those in the high prestige–high skill occupations; those in such occupations were most reluctant to retire.

As a result of his national survey, Louis Harris concluded: "Contrary to widely-held impression, Americans do not contemplate retirement with deep doubts and fears. Instead of thinking that retirement means being put on the shelf, the majority of Americans see it as a chance to lead a different and not unpleasant life."[30]

The finding that a majority of Americans do not dread retirement is only part of the story. The fact is that many of those who look forward to retirement with some anticipation do not find retirement as satisfying as they expected. As an extension of the work done by Friedmann and Havighurst and their colleagues, this author examined the relationship

[29] *Ibid.*, p. 173.
[30] Los Angeles *Times*, November 29, 1965.

between the meaning of work and adjustment to retirement among a group of retired civil service employees.[31] He was able to identify four orientations toward work: 1. There were men who placed a positive, religious value on work, in the spirit of the Protestant Ethic. They constituted a distinct minority (3 of 101 interviewees). 2. There were men who attached positive value to work, but saw no religious significance in it. They stressed creativity and a feeling of purpose as justifications for working. Of the sample, 25 per cent fell in this category. 3. There were men who valued work, but in a negative sense; they tended to see work as a means of keeping out of trouble. The majority fell in this category (61 per cent). 4. There were among the men studied 11 per cent who felt that it was neither necessary nor important for a man to work if he could avoid working.

When white-collar and blue-collar workers were compared, it was found that white-collar workers were more likely to value work positively (29 versus 20 per cent) and less likely to value work negatively (59 versus 64 per cent) or not at all (9 versus 13 per cent). Furthermore, white-collar workers were more satisfied with their former jobs and less enthusiastic about retirement than were the blue-collar workers. In terms of actual adjustment to retirement, moreover, the white-collar workers fared somewhat better than the blue-collar workers. On a scale designed to measure the person's self-concept, it was found that 70 per cent of the white-collar workers had a favorable self-concept in retirement, compared to 48 per cent of the blue-collar workers. On the other hand, 20 per cent of the blue-collar workers had an unfavorable self-concept, compared to 5 per cent of the white-collar workers.

The author remarked:

White-collar and blue-collar workers did not differ significantly in the meanings that they attached to work. The meanings attached to work were related to adjustment, but they did not account for the adjustment differentials between white-collar and blue-collar workers. Such adjustment differentials did exist and were generally in favor of the white-collar workers. How can these differentials be accounted for?

It should be noted that, although white-collar workers expressed greater job satisfaction than that of blue-collar workers and seemed more reluctant to retire voluntarily, they were more likely to have favorable adjustment scores and favorable self-conceptions. Furthermore, they were more likely to say that they missed nothing about work.[32]

[31] Herman J. Loether, "The Meaning of Work and Adjustment to Retirement," in Arthur B. Shostak and William Gomberg, eds., *Blue-Collar World* (Englewood Cliffs, N.J.: Prentice-Hall, Inc., 1964), pp. 517–525.
[32] *Ibid.*, p. 524.

The probable explanation for the differential success between white-collar and blue-collar workers in adapting to retirement is that the factors leading to the white-collar worker's greater identification with and attachment to his occupation also facilitate his adjustment to retirement. White-collar occupations generally require a higher educational level and are inherently more interesting than blue-collar occupations. As a by-product of his higher level of education, the white-collar worker tends to develop greater role flexibility than the blue-collar worker.

The blue-collar worker's job is not really very satisfying to him, but it is all he has; it serves to anchor him to society. Since he does not particularly like his job, he looks forward to retirement. But once he retires, his major tie to society is severed and he has trouble adjusting. He has no adequate substitute for his job.

Because the white-collar worker is more likely to enjoy his job, he is reluctant to leave it and retire. But once he does retire, his greater role flexibility facilitates his adjustment process. He has other activities and interests to substitute for his job.

Thus the blue-collar worker is the more common victim of the retirement trap. The bait that leads him enthusiastically toward retirement is the prospect of leisure and relaxation. But, once in the trap, he is unable to cope with his new-found leisure, because all he knows is how to work. One of the serious problems facing our society is the problem of teaching the average working man how to use his leisure, because the successful use of leisure is the key to successful adjustment to retirement.

Chapter 7. Exploitation of the aged

THERE are many unscrupulous characters who are out to make a dishonest dollar wherever they can get it. Though they do not limit their schemes to the victimization of the elderly, the elderly are their favorite targets. Old people make almost irresistible targets for exploitation, because they represent considerable purchasing power and because they are highly vulnerable.

Although the average yearly income in the 65-and-over category is only $2,530 for a couple and only $1,055 for a person living alone, our older citizens, collectively, have an annual income of about 37 billion dollars. This income comes largely from Social Security payments, pensions, returns on savings and investments, and wages and salaries from full-time or part-time employment.[1] This purchasing power makes our older citizens a highly attractive market, not only for reputable business men but also for confidence men, swindlers, and quacks.

A number of factors explain the particular vulnerability of many older people. For one thing, they generally have small, fixed incomes barely large enough to meet their needs. They are anxious to take advantage of any proposition that promises to provide them with supplementary income, and they are inexperienced or gullible enough to fall for "get rich quick" schemes.

Second, old people frequently live in social isolation and loneliness. They are too naïve to be aware of the many schemes available to part them from their money. Confidence games work precisely because of the victims' naïveté. Lonely old people are frequently taken in by the seeming friendliness and interest shown them by strangers.

Third, many old people become desperate because of illness, pain, or infirmity their doctors cannot help. They are willing to try almost anything promising relief. Moreover, many are constantly in search of the elixir of youth and will submit to almost any torture to remove wrinkles and firm up flabby flesh. Those on the brink of death will pay any cost and go to any

---

[1] President's Council on Aging, *The Older American* (Washington, D.C.: U.S. Government Printing Office, 1963), p. 9; Special Committee on Aging, United States Senate, *Frauds and Deceptions Affecting the Elderly: Investigations, Findings, and Recommendations*, 1964, A Report of the Subcommittee on Frauds and Misrepresentations Affecting the Elderly (Washington, D.C.: U.S. Government Printing Office, 1965), p. v.

lengths to keep lit the spark of life. In a word, countless old people are ripe for the plucking by quacks and food faddists.

Many old people will not admit that they have been victimized, either because they are unaware of the fact or because they do not want to appear foolish. Those who do admit that they have been exploited are often unable to supply the information necessary to apprehend those responsible. And even if the culprits are apprehended, older victims who are forgetful and infirm make very poor witnesses.

Exploitation of the elderly is very difficult to combat. Many of the schemes employed to exploit them are not clearly illegal; they are, rather, on the fringe of the law. There is a very fine line between fraud and sharp business practice. As a matter of fact, in some cases enterprising business men have borrowed practices originated by confidence men and have made them respectable through common usage.

Food fads, health frauds, and quacks

Americans are now paying the greatest price they have ever paid for worthless nostrums, ineffectual and potentially dangerous devices, treatments given by unqualified practitioners, food fads and unneeded diet supplements, and other alluring products or services that make misleading promises of cure or end to pain.

It is incredible that a wealthy nation, priding itself on its enlightenment and its thirst for progress, should pay such a heavy penalty for ignorance or lack of adequate enforcement.

And it is shameful that the elderly of the United States are now clearly the major victims of the highly organized, high-pressure techniques of the modern day medicine man. But this is clearly the case.[2]

It has been estimated that the annual cost of food fads, health frauds, and medical quackery in the United States is about a billion dollars.[3] This is necessarily a very rough estimate, because a large proportion of the exploitation that takes place goes undetected or unreported. The estimated cost of vitamin and health-food quackery alone has been set at about 500 million dollars per year.[4] Because of the particular concern old people show for preserving or restoring their health, they are frequent and substantial contributors to these costs.

Two common pitches used in the sale of vitamin-mineral food supplements and health foods to old people are (1) old people have special nutritional problems which require them to supplement their usual diet,

[2] Special Committee on Aging, United States Senate, *op. cit.*, p. 1.
[3] *Ibid.*, p. 8.
[4] *Ibid.*

and (2) food supplements and health foods prevent or cure various diseases. These premises, both of which are false, are reinforced by articles, books, lectures, and radio programs presented by self-proclaimed nutritional experts.

Fast-talking vitamin salesmen try to convince old people that they are suffering from dietary deficiencies that can be remedied by daily doses of over-priced vitamins. The purchase of vitamin pills creates a serious and unnecessary drain on the incomes of many older people. Furthermore, overdoses of certain vitamins are actually harmful to one's health.

A popular food supplement among food faddists has been seawater. The claim has been made that, since seawater contains numerous minerals and trace elements, it should be taken every day. Seawater thus is bottled and sold to old people at a handsome profit. Actually, the minerals found in seawater are also found in many common foods.

Exotic and expensive health foods and food supplements are sold as effective preventatives or cures for various diseases and infirmities. For example, one food supplement has been presented as the answer to practically all health problems. It presumably cures anemia, arthritis, cancer, diabetes, frigidity, heart trouble, infections, and nervousness. It is said to be beneficial to health, beauty, athletic ability, radiant living, and the capacity to stay young and vital. It even has been implied that this product might help to cure juvenile delinquency.[5]

One of the most serious consequences of health-food quackery among the elderly is that they attempt to cure diseases through special health-food diets and food supplements instead of seeking medical aid. For some this proves to be a fatal mistake.

Most people in the health-food and vitamin industries are sincere and honest business people who make no exaggerated claims for their products. It is the small minority of dishonest operators who create the problems. Health foods have no magical properties, though they are generally as nutritious as any other foods. But they are by no means a necessary part of the diet of old people. In a statement presented to the Senate Subcommittee on Frauds and Misrepresentations Affecting the Elderly, Doctor Frederick J. Stare, Chairman of the Department of Nutrition of the Harvard School of Public Health, said:

Proper eating to provide proper nutrition for oldsters, youngsters, or the middle aged, can be achieved from the wise selection of foods available in ordinary grocery stores. Consuming health foods or dietary supplements is not

[5] Special Committee on Aging, United States Senate, *Health Frauds and Quackery*, Part 2, Hearings before the Subcommittee on Frauds and Misrepresentations Affecting the Elderly, March 9, 1964 (Washington, D.C.: U.S. Government Printing Office, 1964), p. 200.

necessary. For most people these so-called health foods and dietary supplements are a waste of money, and many oldsters have no money to waste. Unfortunately, persons of advancing years are good game for the health hucksters with their phony nutrition advice in books, pamphlets, radio and television.[6]

Because they commonly suffer from chronic illnesses, old people are particularly vulnerable to quacks pushing miracle drugs or mechanical devices guaranteed to cure anything and everything. Frequently, the quack will falsely diagnose some disease such as cancer or heart trouble and then proceed to administer costly treatments designed to "cure" it. The Food and Drug Administration rounded up nearly 1,200 machines called "Micro-Dynameters" which were reputedly capable of diagnosing all kinds of diseases by measuring the minute electrical currents generated by metal attachments applied to the skin. Investigators discovered that all the machine measured was the amount of perspiration present on the skin; if disease was present it did not affect the reading at all. As a matter of fact, the machine worked the same on dead persons as it did on living ones. "Micro-Dynameters" were sold to practitioners for $875 each. Practitioners charged patients $5 to $10 per diagnosis with the machine.[7]

Another device that has been used by medical quacks is an ozone generator recommended for use in the treatment of 47 diseases including tuberculosis, cancer, diabetes, heart disease, and polio. In a three-year period, more than 3,000 ozone generators were sold in the state of California for $150 each. According to authorities, the generator was not only worthless, but it was dangerous because of its output of ozone. The amount of ozone generated was capable of killing mice in a matter of hours.[8]

A report compiled by the Bureau of Food and Drug Inspection of the State of California told how a medical quack made use of a more elaborate version of the same device:

Another larger and more expensive ozone generator known as the cosmic light ozone generator was sold by Franklin D. Lee for $300 each. Lee, a Bakersfield man now serving a 360-day sentence in the Kern County jail for practicing medicine without a license and dispensing misbranded drugs, not

[6] Special Committee on Aging, United States Senate, *Health Frauds and Quackery*, Part 3, Hearings before the Subcommittee on Frauds and Misrepresentations Affecting the Elderly, March 10, 1964 (Washington, D.C.: U.S. Government Printing Office, 1964), p. 299.

[7] Special Committee on Aging, *Health Frauds and Quackery*, Part 2, p. 200.

[8] Special Committee on Aging, United States Senate, *Health Frauds and Quackery*, Part 1, Hearings before the Subcommittee on Frauds and Misrepresentations Affecting the Elderly, January 13, 1964 (Washington, D.C.: U.S. Government Printing Office, 1964), p. 16.

only sold $30,000 worth of these worthless and potentially dangerous devices during a 3-year period but also used them in conjunction with minerals, vitamins, and lotions in giving treatments to hundreds of patients for all kinds of diseases and ailments, including cancer, diabetes, insanity, gallstones, goiters, and varicose veins.[9]

Persons suffering from cancer or arthritis are considered "easy marks" by the unscrupulous because they are desperately seeking help and are often ill-informed about their illness. Phony cancer and arthritis clinics spring up all over the country. They feature pseudoscientific mechanical devices like the ozone generator and so-called miracle drugs. One supposed cancer treatment consisted of distilled water, another of common herbs and weeds.

Arthritis clinics feature such treatments as plunging the affected parts of the body alternately into hot and cold water, drinking alfalfa tea, and lying on beds with trays of uranium ore beneath them. It has been estimated that arthritis victims alone are bilked out of 250 million dollars a year.[10]

The mail order business is a natural one for the health quacks. Many old people are confined to their homes, but they do read newspapers and magazines and they do listen to the radio and watch television. Through these media, the swindlers hustle customers for their products. One so-called cancer cure was sold on a nationwide basis through the mails. It was a "wonder drug" made of wheat, salt, yeast, and water. Prices for the drug ranged from $6.75 to $10.00 per half ounce—a one-week supply. It was supposed to dissolve tumors as well as cure almost anything else you could name.[11]

Large numbers of old and aging people are taken in by rejuvenation schemes. Several types of vibrators have been sold through advertisements claiming the gadgets were effective in removing wrinkles and sagging facial contours. Mud packs, turtle oil, royal jelly, hormone creams, and vitamin lotions have been sold under the guise of rejuvenators. Some quacks subject their victims to long and costly series of injections purported to reverse the aging process. There is no evidence that any device, lotion, or drug is the least bit effective in turning back or even arresting the ravages of time.

Old people are frequently in need of dentures, eyeglasses, a hearing aid, or trusses and other appliances. Because of limited financial resources, ignorance, or fear, they may patronize a quack or order by mail rather than consult a regular dentist, physician, or optometrist. They end up with

[9] Ibid.
[10] Special Committee on Aging, Health Frauds and Quackery, Part 2, p. 219.
[11] Ibid., p. 202.

inferior, poorly fitting appliances, often at higher costs than they would otherwise pay.

There are many so-called dental laboratories, operated by unqualified personnel. They bypass dentists completely and deal directly with the public. Through advertisements, they offer dentures at cut-rate prices. One laboratory was selling a complete set of dentures for $35. The elderly are a prime target. An American Dental Association survey in 1961 found that 78.3 per cent of Americans past the age of 60 wear dentures or bridges. The average price those surveyed had paid to dentists was $104.21 for complete upper dentures, and $100 for complete lowers. In comparison, those who bought their dentures from quacks payed an average of $82.50 for uppers and $71.88 for lowers.[12] Thus, for a few dollars less, these people subjected themselves to unprofessional care. Furthermore, 12.1 per cent of those surveyed believed that they could get satisfactory false teeth directly from a dental laboratory technician or an unlicensed person.[13]

The seriousness of the problem of dental quacks has been stressed by the American Dental Association:

Artificial teeth or dentures can never serve a person as well as can his healthy natural teeth. Natural teeth, with proper personal and professional care, should last a lifetime. However, as a result of neglect, disease or injury, many people need partial or full-mouth dentures. The skills and knowledge of a dentist are required to provide dentures that will restore and maintain the harmony and appearance of the face as well as assure the proper alignment of the teeth. A person lacking natural teeth and not properly fitted with dentures will be forced to restrict his diet in a way not consonant with good, general health.

In some communities, there are unqualified persons who operate contrary to laws designed to protect the health of the public that permit only qualified, duly licensed dentists to practice dentistry. Many of these illegal operators advertise to the public, as do most health quacks. Others depend on word-of-mouth advertising to bring customers to their door. They say there is no need to see a "middle man," the dentist. They promise rapid service and a perfect fit. Many unsuspecting people, hoping to save money, have been trapped by such false advertisements. The tragic fact is that the person is not properly cared for, suffers a needless amount of discomfort and even pain, often suffers injury to his gums and surrounding tissues and certainly saves no money since, in the end, professional care is necessary to restore his oral health and to then fit him properly with dentures.[14]

Another lucrative area for swindlers is the sale of hearing aids. Exorbitant prices are charged for hearing aids by unscrupulous salesmen. One

[12] Special Committee on Aging, *Health Frauds and Quackery*, Part 3, p. 325.
[13] *Ibid.*, p. 327.
[14] *Ibid.*, p. 325.

elderly lady was charged $700 for her hearing aid and $600 for a special hearing device for her television set. It is not unusual for a fast-talking salesman to sell an older person two hearing aids, one for each ear, when one would suffice.[15]

During the period when the 1960 census was being taken, enterprising swindlers canvassed a Los Angeles neighborhood populated largely by old people. The swindlers passed themselves off as census enumerators, gathered information about the health problems of the elderly citizens, then launched an all-out campaign to sell hearing aids and other appliances. When the legitimate census takers did appear in the neighborhood they met with resistance from the inhabitants, who suspected them of being swindlers.

Eyeglasses sold through the mail frequently contain improperly ground lenses. One advertiser claimed that the lenses of the eyeglasses he sold were ground according to prescriptions. Experts testified that 10 of every 15 pairs of such glasses examined were improperly ground.[16] Other eyeglasses have been mounted in highly flammable plastic frames.

Elderly people suffering from hernias are also subject to exploitation. A former used car salesman who was a self-proclaimed specialist in the treatment of hernias advertised that he had invented a device that would give instant relief from rupture trouble. He fitted his victims with trusses worth $3.90 and charged $75.00. He was arrested for false advertising and practicing medicine without a license.[17]

Recognizing the magnitude of the food-fad, health-fraud, and medical-quackery problems facing the elderly, the Senate's Special Committee on Aging held extensive hearings in 1964 to explore possible remedies and suggest needed legislation. During the course of the hearings George P. Larrick, then Commissioner of Food and Drugs of the U.S. Department of Health, Education, and Welfare, offered a four-point program aimed at the elimination of quackery:

1. Improvement in the quality and quantity of medical care.
2. More research to find effective means for the prevention and treatment of disease.
3. Enactment of stronger laws against quackery and more effective enforcement of such laws.
4. Education of the public. "The well-informed consumer is much less likely

[15] Special Committee on Aging, *Health Frauds and Quackery*, Part 2, p. 168.
[16] Special Committee on Aging, United States Senate, *Health Frauds and Quackery*, Part 4A (Eye Care), Hearings before the Subcommittee on Frauds and Misrepresentations Affecting the Elderly, April 6, 1964 (Washington, D.C.: U.S. Government Printing Office, 1964), p. 349.
[17] Special Committee on Aging, *Health Frauds and Quackery*, Part 1, p. 22.

to make unwise choices in health products and services than the person who lacks basic knowledge of these matters."[18]

Confidence games and frauds

It is difficult to determine the total annual "take" from confidence games and frauds, because only about 2 per cent of the victims file complaints. However, a conservative estimate places the annual loss at about 4 billion dollars.[19]

The confidence man is a student of human nature. He is astute at sizing up his victims and picking out their points of greatest vulnerability. He is adept at misrepresenting himself, his schemes, or his products so as to befuddle his victims into actions that are against their better judgment. Once the victims realize they have been fleeced (if they ever do), they often feel too embarrassed to file complaints with the authorities. Because of their particular vulnerabilities, old people are often the favorite victims of confidence men. Some old people, as a matter of fact, fall prey to swindlers repeatedly. Their names are sometimes circulated from one confidence man to another.

There are many confidence games in common use, and more are being invented all the time. Though old people fall prey to all kinds of confidence games, many games are not directed particularly toward nor limited to older victims. People of all ages are taken in by fast-talking swindlers "selling" dance lessons, magazine subscriptions, aluminum siding, fertilizer, health insurance, and so on. Phony mail order schemes to "earn money in your own home" or to get rich overnight through vending-machine franchises bilk victims from the pre-teens through the eighties. Some schemes, however, are deliberately pitched toward the elderly, and it is to these schemes we will devote our attention in the following pages.

Numerous elderly women have fallen victim to a scheme that originated in Canada in 1963. In the last quarter of 1965, 38 elderly women in the Los Angeles area were bilked out of $200,000 through the "bank examiner" scheme.[20] This swindle works this way: A man calls an elderly woman on the telephone and identifies himself as a bank examiner. He tells her that someone is believed to be tampering with her bank account and asks her to aid in the apprehension of the culprit. She is instructed to go to the bank and withdraw all of her money, which she does. After she returns home

[18] Special Committee on Aging, *Health Frauds and Quackery*, Part 2, p. 203.
[19] Interview with Lieutenant G. G. Greeley, Sergeant J. P. Lovretovich, and Sergeant R. D. Mercer, Los Angeles Police Department, January 6, 1966.
[20] *Citizen News*, Los Angeles, December 9, 1965.

with her money, she gets another call from the bank examiner, who informs her that the plan worked and that the teller who had been tampering with her account has been caught. The bank examiner thanks her for her cooperation and tells her that, rather than inconvenience her so late in the day, he will send a bank messenger to her house to pick up her money and return it to the bank. The bank messenger shows up, collects the money, gives her an official-looking receipt, and disappears. This swindle is used almost exclusively on elderly women who live alone. The youngest victim among the Los Angeles women was 58; most of them were in their seventies.

Older people who dream of spending their last days in some pleasant, far-off spot like Hawaii, Florida, California, or Arizona are sitting ducks for the sharks in the mail order–land sale business. Land is sold through misleading advertisements which make the location sound like paradise. Low down payments and low monthly payments put these *bargain lots* within the reach of the limited incomes of older people. As Mr. Kenneth B. Willson of the Better Business Bureau said at the Senate hearings in 1963,

Homesites purchasable on a $10 down, $10 monthly basis have a particular appeal to those on limited Social Security or retirement incomes. High-pressure sales campaigns conducted in cities far distant from the developments, supported by illustrative advertising matter grossly distorting the true nature of the land offered as it now exists have induced many old people in this income group to buy lots in remote, desolate areas, lacking in roads, utilities, neighbors, schools, stores, or any other evidence of civilization. Deception results not only from misrepresentation, but from the failure of the promoter to disclose the real character of the land and its location.[21]

Many dream lots in Hawaii are on the slopes of active volcanoes, those in Florida are sometimes under water, and those in the southwest are often in the midst of desert wastelands. In some locations it is necessary to bring water in by truck. Distances are often misrepresented. Facilities said to be minutes away are often hours away.

The "free lot" gimmick is often used to sell land. The victim is informed that he has won a free lot and has only to pay closing costs ranging from $30 to $90. However, it turns out that the free lot is so narrow that it is not usable. Therefore, the promoter seeks to sell the "lucky winner" an adjoining lot so that he will have an "estate."

Elderly people have been victimized by a number of state-chartered and

---

[21] Special Committee on Aging, United States Senate, *Frauds and Quackery Affecting the Older Citizen*, Part 2, January 16, 1963 (Washington, D.C.: U.S. Government Printing Office, 1963), p. 148.

privately insured savings and loan companies. Several of these companies were operating in Maryland from 1958 to 1961. They advertised nationally that they would pay extremely high interest rates on savings. In addition, they promised expensive gifts to new savers. The officers of many of these companies were indicted on charges of embezzlement, larceny, and conspiracy to defraud and the companies went bankrupt, wiping out the life savings of many victims.[22]

Confidence men frequently take advantage of Social Security beneficiaries by impersonating Social Security agents and extorting money from elderly victims. This is done by promising the victims that their monthly benefits will be increased upon payment of a fee to the agent; by persuading the victims to pay a fee to the agent to guarantee continuation of benefits; or by creating a fictitious overpayment to the victims and having them return the money to the agent. Two swindlers approached two elderly men, aged 86 and 84, and told them that they were Social Security agents. They told the men that they had been overpaid and they, the agents, would collect the overpayments and return them to the Social Security Administration. One of the victims turned over $750 to the swindlers. The other told the swindlers he didn't have the $1,628 demanded of him, but would get it for them the next day. Instead, he reported the matter to the Social Security office and the swindlers were arrested.[23]

Swindlers had a heyday in the months between the time the Medicare Program was enacted by Congress and the time it went into effect on July 1, 1966. Posing as Social Security agents, they called on elderly persons whose names and addresses they had presumably found in commercial mailing lists. The victims were told that the "agents" were calling on them to explain the Medicare provisions to them. The swindlers did supply their victims with a certain amount of information and with brochures they had picked up at Social Security offices. However, they also told their victims they could obtain a special discount on Medicare Insurance premiums if they signed up early and paid their initial premiums in advance. The "agents" collected as many advance premiums as they could and pocketed them.[24]

Another area in which old people are particularly susceptible is sales of pre-need burial services. Though many of the pre-need plans being sold are legitimate, there is a small number of dishonest promoters at large. They

---

[22] *Ibid.*, p. 163.

[23] Special Committee on Aging, United States Senate, *Frauds and Quackery Affecting the Older Citizen*, Part 3, January 17, 1963 (Washington, D.C.: U.S. Government Printing Office, 1963), p. 498.

[24] Los Angeles *Times*, August 19, 1965.

seek to persuade the elderly to purchase complete burial services in advance, to make sure that expenses will be covered at the time of death, and as a hedge against inflation. The contracts sold are misrepresented to the purchasers. The impression is given that the cost covers everything involved when, in fact, it may cover only the cost of the casket. One salesman explained the wording of the contract by telling an aged couple that when funeral directors say casket they mean the complete service. Customers have also been told that their burial service is good for the funeral home of their choice when, in fact, it may not be honored by any funeral home. The money collected by these promoters is supposed to be held in trust until such time as it is needed; instead, it is often pocketed.

Even in those cases in which the complete burial service is provided as promised, there is some question whether pre-need plans are desirable. The National Funeral Directors Association has taken the position that such plans are not desirable because of the interest lost during the years between the time of payment for the burial service and the time of death. Howard C. Raether, then Executive Secretary of the National Funeral Directors Association, told the Senate Special Committee on Aging:

One of many examples of what the purchase of a "funeral" and/or "funeral" merchandise can needlessly cost is the Julesburg, Colo., contract calling for the advance purchase of two caskets, two vaults, and a gravestone for $1,650. In 10 years if this money were placed in a savings account at the rate of interest paid in Julesburg (compounded semiannually) it would earn $810.44. Therefore, if the merchandise was not needed for 10 years—it would cost not $1,650 but $2,460.44. And, no matter when death occurred whatever the cost for the merchandise might be, no services are included. Someone would have to be called to care for the body and provide the facilities, equipment, and personnel for the funeral services.[25]

The point of the hearings on frauds and deceptions affecting the elderly by the Senate Special Committee on Aging was to discover just what the most pressing problems were and to make recommendations that would help solve the problems. The conclusion reached was that steps should be taken (1) to regulate those activities deemed not to be in the best interest of the elderly, and (2) to educate the public to the various schemes used by disreputable persons, as a defense against exploitation. In the summary report of the Subcommittee on Frauds and Misrepresentations Affecting the Elderly, the Subcommittee Chairman, Senator Harrison A. Williams, said:

[25] Special Committee on Aging, United States Senate, *Preneed Burial Service*, Hearing before the Subcommittee on Frauds and Misrepresentations Affecting the Elderly, May 19, 1964 (Washington, D.C.: U. S. Government Printing Office, 1964), p. 19.

The subcommittee has no desire to add needless legislation to the lawbooks; neither do we propose to ignore obvious gaps in our present regulatory structure. The subcommittee also realizes that education, public and private, can often be more effective than regulatory action. In the following pages, the subcommittee makes recommendations that attempt to give at least as much attention to education as to law enforcement.[26]

Many of the schemes used to exploit the elderly are clearly violations of the law. These violations can be handled through efficient law enforcement practices. Also, such swindles can often be prevented by far-ranging educational programs. Local law enforcement agencies often do so through public lectures, wide circulation of pamphlets and warnings through various news media.

On the fringe

In many cases, the types of exploitation to which old people are subjected are not clearly violations of the law. Many of the commonly used schemes are in those fringe areas lying between sharp business practice and outright fraud. Much of credit buying falls into this area. There is no outright violation of the law, but interest rates are seldom presented in a forthright manner. Much advertising also falls into the fringe area. The federal government must be a constant watchdog over advertisers to see that they do not make unsubstantiated claims for their products.

It is in this fringe area that law enforcement agencies are of little help. Only when public indignation is aroused is it possible to squelch fringe practices. But the public becomes aroused only when practices not in its best interests are exposed. It seems that the logical solution is a well-informed and wary public, able to distinguish between the sound and the unsound business proposition. As Senator Williams has pointed out, education deserves as much attention as law enforcement.

[26] Special Committee on Aging, *Frauds and Deceptions Affecting the Elderly: Investigations, Findings, and Recommendations*, 1964, p. vi.

Chapter 8. Death

REGARDLESS of one's social station, one cannot avoid the eventual reality of death. The famous man enjoys no advantage over the most insignificant member of society when his time to die arrives. In spite of the age-old dream of immortality, the "Grim Reaper" has never been denied. Medical advances can serve to postpone the inevitable, but they do not offer any prospects of avoiding it. Although the life expectancy in the United States has been slowly but steadily increasing, as it approaches the natural life span it must come to a halt. No one is sure just what the life span (the maximum length of life barring accident or disease) is. Guesses place it at anywhere from 100 to 120 years.[1] There have presumably been cases of persons living to 150, but these have been rare indeed. Obviously, life expectancy has not yet reached the life span, but each additional year added to life expectancy comes a little harder.

Even now, life expectancy in the United States has reached a point where the elimination of most of our leading causes of death would have relatively little impact. It has been estimated that the elimination of heart disease would increase the life expectancy by only four years; elimination of stroke, by one year; and elimination of cancer, by two years.[2]

Although more Americans are living to the age of 60 than ever before, the life expectancy of those reaching the age of 60 in 1958 was not much different from that of those who reached 60 in 1781. It has been estimated that the life expectancy of males of age 60 in 1781 was about 14.8 years, compared to 15.6 years for those reaching 60 in 1958. Females reaching 60 in 1781 could anticipate about 16.1 years of life, compared to 19 years for those reaching 60 in 1958.[3] Furthermore, these life expectancies have changed little since 1958.

Death is a process rather than an event. From the day we are born (or

---

[1] Ralph Thomlinson, *Population Dynamics: Causes and Consequences of World Demographic Change* (New York: Random House, Inc., 1965), p. 120.

[2] Reubin Andres, "Expectations for Extension of Longevity," paper presented at the annual meeting of the Western Gerontological Society, Los Angeles, Calif., November 13, 1965.

[3] Isaac Asimov, *The Intelligent Man's Guide to Science*, Vol. II: *The Biological Sciences* (New York: Basic Books, Inc., 1960), p. 649; U.S. Bureau of the Census, *Statistical Abstract of the United States, 1961* (82d ed.; Washington, D.C., 1961), table 55, p. 55.

even before) we begin the very gradual, but inevitable process of dying. Intimately related to the process of dying is the process of aging. As the body ages, it approaches ever more closely the state of death. We treat death as though it were an event. When certain of the major bodily processes, such as respiration and circulation, cease, we declare the person dead. Other bodily processes, however, may cease prior to the cessation of respiration and circulation, and still others may continue on afterward. From a biological standpoint, it is very difficult to fix a time of death. Time of death is, in fact, socially defined and medically verified by a licensed physician.

The social aspects of the definition of death can be better appreciated by a consideration of the ceremony that has traditionally marked the death of a pope. The word of a physician is not sufficient to declare a pope dead. The Cardinal Camerlengo must ceremonially verify that the pope is, indeed, dead.

Until the end of the nineteenth century, accompanied by the Master of Ceremonies and by Cardinals residing in Rome, the Camerlengo approached the bed holding a small silver hammer in his right hand. Gently he lifted from the face of the Pope the linen that covered it. While all present kneeled, the Camerlengo prayed. Then in a clear voice he pronounced the Pope's family name and baptismal name. When the cold lips failed to answer, he touched the Pope's forehead with the silver hammer. Three times, in the profoundly silent room, he called the Pope's name and the little hammer tapped the cold forehead. Then he turned to those present and solemnly declared: "The Pope is truly dead." Notaries, the Master of Ceremonies and physicians signed the certificate of death. The Camerlengo signed it too and put his seal on it.

Since the end of the nineteenth century the use of the silver hammer has been abandoned. The rest of the ceremony to certify the death is the same.[4]

In general, the practice is to let a physician establish the time of death. Nevertheless, the time of death set by the physician is a judgment on his part rather than an established fact. When President Kennedy was assassinated, physicians continued to work over his body and succeeded in keeping his heart beating for a time, although, for all intents and purposes, he could have been considered dead. His life was considered so valuable that the physicians took measures that might have been considered extraordinary in other circumstances.

Many cases have been reported in which patients, who are—to all appearances—dead, are revived by the persistent efforts of physicians. There is a very fine line between life and death—a blurred line, at that.

[4] Zsolt Aradi, *The Popes: The History of How They Are Chosen, Elected and Crowned* (New York: Collier Books, Inc., 1962), p. 34.

In many societies death is accepted as a natural occurrence. People of all ages have the opportunity to observe the process of dying and the presence of death. In traditional China, death did not represent the end of life. Rather, it represented a change in status from living family member to ancestor. In a sense it represented a promotion, for ancestors were held in high esteem. Societies ravaged by pestilence, famine, and war become intimately familiar with the phenomenon of death. When death becomes commonplace, it loses much of its mystery; it is frequently accepted as an integral part of the life cycle. There is no necessity, or attempt made, to hide the fact of death.

In our own society, there is an avoidance of and denial of death. Death is not a proper subject for a polite conversation. As Fulton says,

In America today we have come to a point in our history when we are beginning to react to death as we would to a communicable disease. Death no longer is viewed as the price of moral trespass or as the result of theological wrath; rather, in our modern secular world, death is coming to be seen as the consequence of personal neglect or untoward accident. Death is now a temporal matter. Like cancer or syphilis, it is a private disaster that we discuss only reluctantly with our physician. Moreover, as in the manner of many contagious diseases, those who are caught in the throes of death are isolated from their fellow human beings, while those who have succumbed to it are hidden quickly from view. The aged, those most susceptible to death, seek in ever-increasing numbers to remove themselves to segregated retirement communities, there to await fate in the same manner as the leper once did. Death, like a noxious disease, has become a taboo subject, and as such it is both the object of much disguise and denial as well as of raucous and macabre humor.[5]

Desperately, men seek ways to avoid, or at least postpone, their deaths. The prospect that cures for many fatal diseases are in the offing has led to the suggestion that the deceased be put into deep freeze immediately after death and be kept there until such time as it is possible to defrost and revive him. It has also been suggested that terminal patients be frozen before death until such time as their maladies can be cured. At the time of this writing no one has been frozen; the prospect of such action, however, leads to interesting speculation about the moral and legal problems involved. What would be the status of the frozen person's soul? Would the soul also be in a state of suspension? What legal rights would the frozen person have? Would he retain the rights to his estate? Who would be liable for his debts? Would someone have to file income tax forms in his behalf?

[5] Robert Fulton, Introduction in Robert Fulton, ed., *Death and Identity* (New York: John Wiley & Sons, Inc., 1965), p. 4.

It is highly unlikely that man will ever be successful in his search for the secret of immortality. Practically speaking, the attainment of immortality would be a major catastrophe. There is serious concern over the "population explosion." If no one were to die, in a very short time men would be crowded, shoulder to shoulder, over every available inch of the earth. The dramatic increase in life expectancy is largely responsible for the present serious rate of world population growth. It is paradoxical that, through man's well-meaning attempts to preserve life, a very real threat to his survival as a species has been created.

Approximately 1.8 million Americans are dying each year. This amounts to a death rate of 9.5 per 1,000 of the population.[6] Although the long-range trend in the death rate is downward, the increasing numbers of older persons in the population will eventually reverse this trend. The more older persons there are, the more deaths there will be. The 1960 death rate for those between 65 and 74 years of age was 41.2 per 1,000; for those between 75 and 84, 87; and for those 85 and over, 209.6.[7] The social and social psychological problems associated with death are already serious and will become increasingly more serious in the future.

Personal aspects of death

Every man must, sooner or later, face up to the fact of his own death. Young people are usually far enough removed in time from death to be able to disassociate themselves from it. Since the tendency in American society is to hide death as much as possible, it is not unusual for a person to live for many years without having any direct contact with death. The mass media, as a matter of course, report the deaths of famous people. However, deaths of particular people, not known on a personal basis, seldom have much impact on an individual.

The possibility of one's own death is most likely to enter awareness when one's relatives or friends die. Particularly when acquaintances of one's own age die, one is likely to begin thinking about death in more personal terms. Naturally, there are considerable individual differences in the times at which persons begin thinking about death. However, most persons by their middle thirties have given some thought to their impending deaths.

Common reactions to thoughts about death are feelings of fear or dread. Death represents the unknown, and fear of the unknown is widespread.

[6] *Statistical Abstract, op. cit.,* table 58, p. 58.
[7] *Ibid.*

Herman Feifel studied the attitudes toward death of three groups of persons: 85 mentally ill patients with a mean age of 36; 40 older people with a mean age of 67; and 85 "normals" consisting of 50 young people with a mean age of 26 and 35 professional people with a mean age of 40.[8] He asked them during which age periods they thought people fear death most and least. He found that patients and older people selected the period of the seventies as the time when people most fear death, because they are so close to it. The "normals" felt that people in their forties and fifties feared death the most because by those ages it was becoming a definite possibility and because those ages marked the period at which accomplishment and reproductive capacity were on the wane.[9]

The usual response was that childhood was the period during which there was the least fear of death. However, the older people frequently singled out the seventies as the period during which death was least feared. They felt that persons in their seventies had lived their lives and were able to resign themselves to death.[10] Feifel reports that there is a high correlation between a person's own attitudes toward death and the attitudes he attributes to others. Therefore, it can be implied that the subjects' responses to these questions were representative of their own feelings about death.

There is reason to believe that large numbers of older persons resign themselves to the possibility of their deaths. Wendell K. Swenson studied the attitudes toward death of more than 200 persons 60 years of age or older. His subjects were obtained from three separate sources: homes for the aged, golden age clubs, and industries and companies employing older people.[11] Swenson found that he was able to identify three separate categories of people according to their attitudes toward death. Of his subjects, 45 per cent admitted they looked forward to death, 44 per cent indicated that they preferred not to think about death, and 10 per cent admitted that they feared death. Persons who engaged in frequent religious activity or demonstrated a high degree of religiosity tended to look forward to death more frequently than persons who were not religious. Also, persons who resided in homes for the aged viewed death more positively than those who lived with their spouses or alone.[12]

Apparently, as a person grows older he becomes more conscious of the

[8] "Attitudes toward Death in Some Normal and Mentally Ill Populations," in Herman Feifel, ed., *The Meaning of Death* (New York: McGraw-Hill Book Company, Inc., 1959), pp. 114–130.

[9] *Ibid.*, p. 118.

[10] *Ibid.*

[11] "Attitudes toward Death Among the Aged," *Minnesota Medicine*, XLII (1959), pp. 399–402, reprinted in Fulton, *op. cit.*, pp. 105–111.

[12] *Ibid.*, pp. 108–109.

fact that one day he must die. He is not likely to ever become enthusiastic about the prospect, but he may gradually resign himself to his fate. Some people, even on their deathbeds, are unable to accept the fact that it can happen and is happening to them. Most people, however, are able to make some kind of adjustment to the idea.

Swenson's finding that religious people were more likely to look forward to death than nonreligious people serves to illuminate the two predominant, but contrasting, views of death held by Americans. People who are not religious commonly see death as the end of everything—the extinction of the self. Religious people tend to see death as the gateway to the afterlife; immortality is seen as an aftermath of death. Religion offers the prospect of eternal peace in heaven or some other paradise in the "world beyond." Christianity and many other religions teach that life is merely an imperfect preliminary to the perfect afterlife.

In his study, Feifel found that the religious person was personally more afraid of death than the nonreligious person.[13] The nonreligious person feared death because it meant the termination of life or because he was concerned about the welfare of his family. In addition to these reasons, the religious person also worried about his own salvation. Even those religious persons who were confident that they were going to heaven rather than hell frequently harbored personal fears of death.

Some of those subjects in Feifel's study who were judged to be most religious were also most afraid of death.[14] This finding points up the fact that people frequently turn to religion as a refuge from the finality of death. There is a tendency for religiosity to become more common as people age. People who are not particularly religious in their younger years may become devout as they grow older. For many people, their religious fervor appears to stem from their fear of death. Religion, however, seems to be most comforting and reassuring to those who come to it through faith rather than through fear of death.

Ill health and infirmity help prepare people for death. Persons whose health is poor are more likely to look forward to death than those who are in good health.[15] The more pain and discomfort there is connected with an illness, the more the aging person is likely to welcome the prospect of death. Increasing infirmity has consequences similar to those of illness. W. Somerset Maugham, who was deaf and going blind when he died at the age of 91, said, "I am sick of this way of life. The weariness and sadness of old age make it intolerable."[16]

[13] *Op. cit.*, pp. 121–122.
[14] *Ibid.*, p. 122.
[15] Swenson, *op. cit.*
[16] *South Bay Daily Breeze*, Torrance, Calif., December 13, 1965.

A distinction should be made between the fear of dying and the fear of death. Many people tend to be more concerned with the process of dying than they are with death itself. They are concerned with the circumstances of their deaths. They dread the thought of suffering and pain. Feifel asked his subjects to state their preferences as to the manner, place, and time of their deaths.[17] The overwhelming majority wished to die quickly and with a minimum of suffering. They frequently expressed a desire to die peacefully in their sleep. It was commonly felt that a heart attack would be a quick, easy way to go. The majority of the subjects stated that they preferred to die at home in bed. The preferred time of death was at night, because it was felt that that was the time that would least inconvenience others.

Dying at home is becoming an ever more rare occurrence. More than 50 per cent of the people who die each year die in a hospital. The percentage of older people who die in hospitals is undoubtedly higher than it is for the total population because of their higher rate of hospitalization. Occasionally, dying patients are released from hospitals so that they may go home to die. But usually they die in the hospital.

A particularly poignant social problem is the management of the process of dying. Doctors are constantly plagued by the question of whether they should inform a patient that he is dying. One side of the argument is that informing the patient of his impending death merely subjects him to psychological torment. Doctor S. L. Wilens takes the position that the patient should not be told:

"But what good is achieved in detecting a disease process that can neither be cured nor significantly modified by medical therapy?" All the doctor does when he tells the man is give him a psychological torment "that will afflict him for the rest of his days."

And often enough people with these sleeping incurable diseases will outlive both the doctors who discovered them and their healthy contemporaries in whom medical science can find no sleepers.[18]

The other side of the argument is that the patient should be told in order to make the most of the time he has left and in order to make plans for his family and get his affairs in order. Ideally, the doctor is supposed to decide in each individual case whether the patient wants to know that he is going to die, and whether the patient is able to make an acceptable adjustment to the news. According to Feifel, however, anywhere from 69

[17] *Op. cit.*, pp. 119–120.
[18] Los Angeles *Times*, January 3, 1966.

to 90 per cent of doctors prefer not to tell their patients that they are dying.[19]

In their book, *Awareness of Dying*, Glaser and Strauss discuss four types of *awareness contexts* involving terminal patients, members of hospital staffs, and members of the patients' families.[20] The first context they call *closed awareness*. This refers to the situation in which the patient is unaware of the fatal nature of his illness. The news is kept from him by staff members and by members of his family. Those who are aware of the patient's situation must do their best to guard the secret. Obviously, closed awareness puts considerable strain upon the interpersonal relations between those who are aware and the unaware patient.

The second awareness context is a highly unstable one called *suspicion awareness*. In this situation the patient suspects that he is dying and attempts to confirm his suspicions. Meanwhile others try to keep the news from him. Glaser and Strauss say:

> How does a patient who suspects that he is dying try to verify his suspicions while others, who recognize that he suspects, simultaneously attempt to negate his suspicions? The hallmark of this awareness context is that the patient does not know, but only suspects with varying degrees of certainty, that the hospital personnel believe him to be dying. The consequential interaction—to run a bit ahead of the story—can be described metaphorically as a fencing match, wherein the patient is on the offensive and staff members are carefully and cannily on the defensive. Under conditions of closed awareness there was little contest for interactional control; now a contest between patient and staff is characteristic.[21]

The third type of awareness context is *mutual pretense awareness*. In this case the patient knows that he is dying and the staff and family members know, but everyone avoids discussing the subject or pretends that death is not imminent.

The fourth type of awareness context is *open awareness*. In the open awareness context everyone involved knows that the patient is dying. The crucial question here is how the patient is able to handle his awareness. Does he panic at the thought of death and become a problem to hospital staff and family? Or, does he accept the fact and handle it in some acceptable manner? There is reason to believe that older patients are better prepared to face the prospect of death and, therefore, are more likely to manage the process of dying in an acceptable manner.

[19] Herman Feifel, "Death," in Norman L. Farberow, ed., *Taboo Topics* (New York: Atherton Press, 1963), p. 17.

[20] Barney G. Glaser and Anselm L. Strauss (Chicago: Aldine Publishing Company, Inc., 1965).

[21] *Ibid.*, p. 47.

Glaser and Strauss make the important point that dying is not just a personal matter; it is definitely social. A fatally ill college professor, when asked by a colleague if there was anything that he could do to help, responded, "No, I guess not. Dying is a family matter." With the ever increasing number of people who are dying in hospitals, dying is now frequently more than a family matter. It is a matter in which hospital staff members are also intimately involved.

Social aspects of death

Since each person is a participant in a number of social systems, the termination of his participation through death tends to disrupt the systems. The extent to which a system is disrupted by the death of a participant depends upon the nature of the system and the particular role that the deceased played in the system.

A large, impersonal system like General Motors is not likely to be disrupted to any appreciable extent by the death of a semiskilled factory worker. On the other hand, the death of the president of the company may disrupt the system, at least temporarily. Recognizing this fact, insurance companies have introduced their "key man" policies and have had considerable success in selling them to corporations.

A small, personal system like a family is likely to be seriously disrupted for a considerable length of time by the loss of any member. Individual role players are of considerable importance to the family unit and are usually difficult to replace. It is much easier for General Motors to replace the deceased factory worker than it is for the Smith family to find a new husband and father. In many cases deceased family members are never replaced; the social system of the family is permanently altered by their deaths. Even before death has occurred, the imminence of death is bound to have profound effects upon the family. Knowledge that a husband has a fatal disease changes the whole course of family activity. Plans for the future must be altered or abandoned. Those plans that include the dying person must be replaced by plans that omit him.

The fatal illness itself greatly alters the pattern of family activity. If the dying person is bedridden, much family activity will be devoted to his care. If the person is hospitalized, other members of the family will need to make frequent trips to the hospital. As the end nears, much activity by other members of the family will be curtailed so that they will be available for final good-byes. Patients who linger beyond the expected time of death may put great stress upon the family. Sometimes the stress is so great that there is a feeling of relief when the death finally occurs.

If the stricken member of the family is unaware of his impending death, the stress upon the family will be even more severe. Family members will undoubtedly find it difficult to interact with the dying member without revealing what they know. Keeping up the pretense that the dying person will recover and resume an active family role can be both physically and mentally fatiguing. Even in the case where the stricken member of the family is aware of his plight, the strain accompanying social interaction is likely to be great. It is practically impossible to interact with the dying person on the same basis that interaction took place prior to the knowledge of the fatal affliction. In times of such crisis, family relations are often strained almost to the breaking point.

When death finally comes to the ailing family member, a whole new series of tension-producing situations faces the family. Someone must take responsibility for making the necessary arrangements for burial or cremation. Unpleasant decisions must be made, and distasteful business must be conducted at the time when grief is most acute. Frequently, members of the immediate family are just not able to handle the arrangements; a more distant member of the family or a friend may be relied upon.

Societal pressures dictate the kind of memorial services to be conducted for the deceased. The day of the large, elaborate funeral is passing. Nevertheless, a certain amount of ceremony must be tolerated. An attempt to dispense with ceremony altogether will be rebuffed as a sign of lack of respect for the dead. Family members will be admonished to "do what is right by their dead."

As a normal consequence of the death of a close relative, family members are stricken with grief. According to Erich Lindemann, the bereaved are marked by a remarkably uniform set of reactions.[22] He found in interviews with 101 bereaved persons that these included:

. . . (1) sensations of somatic distress, which included a feeling of tightness in the throat, choking or shortness of breath, need for sighing and an empty feeling in the abdomen, lack of muscular power, and an intensive subjective distress described as tension or mental pain; (2) intense preoccupation with the image of the deceased; (3) strong feelings of guilt; (4) a loss of warmth toward others with a tendency to respond with irritability and anger; and finally, (5) disoriented behavior patterns.[23]

[22] "Symptomatology and Management of Acute Grief," *American Journal of Psychiatry*, CI (1944), pp. 141–148, reprinted in Robert Fulton, ed., *Death and Identity*, pp. 186–201.

[23] Fulton, *op. cit.*, pp. 181–182.

Lindemann says:

The duration of the grief reaction seems to depend upon the success with which a person does the *grief work*, namely, emancipation from the bondage of the deceased, readjustment to the environment in which the deceased is missing, and the formation of new relationships. One of the big obstacles to this work seems to be the fact that many patients try to avoid the intense distress connected with the grief experience and to avoid the expression of emotion necessary for it.[24]

Lindemann implies that the bereaved survivors must suffer through the distress that accompanies grief before they can leave their grief behind them. Those who fight the grief syndrome do not avoid it; they merely delay it.

The persons interviewed by Lindemann came from all age categories. Therefore, it might be assumed that the reactions observed by Lindemann would be observed in the same form among older persons. Stern, Williams, and Prados, however, discovered different grief reactions in 25 older subjects, ranging in age from 53 to 70.[25] Interestingly enough, it was found that these older people seldom displayed overt mental manifestations of grief or guilt feelings; their grief reactions primarily took the form of somatic illness. Moreover, the subjects tended to glorify the image of the deceased and to isolate themselves from other members of the family. The contact they did have with other members of the family could best be described as hostile. Perhaps the differences in the grief syndrome of these older people and the syndrome described by Lindemann can be explained in terms of the different perspective the older person has of death. Older people may see the death of a spouse less as a personal loss than as a pointed reminder that one's own death is not far off. The older person may come to accept the fact that the spouse is likely to die and, thus, be better able to adjust to the time when he himself is dying. A significant fact that would seem to support this line of reasoning is that an older parent is generally harder hit by the death of a child than by the death of a spouse.

Part of the process of recovery from grief depends upon the reestablishment of social relationships with other people. The bereaved status increases the difficulty of reestablishing such relationships. Acquaintances of the bereaved often find it awkward and embarrassing to speak to him; consequently, they may avoid him. They may feel that they should say something about the deceased, or offer their condolences, but they may fear

[24] Fulton, *op. cit.*, p. 190.
[25] Karl Stern, Gwendolyn M. Williams, and Miguel Prados, "Grief Reactions in Later Life, *American Journal of Psychiatry*, LVIII (1951), pp. 289–294, reprinted in Fulton, *op. cit.*, pp. 240–249.

the reawakening of feelings of grief in the survivor. In effect, a forced isolation accompanies bereavement and hampers the return to an altered but more normal routine of life.

The older person who has lost a spouse is faced with the necessity of reorganizing his life pattern. One of the major role players, and perhaps the only other role player, in his family social system has been lost. He may reorganize the system without the spouse or he may attempt to find a substitute. It is not unusual for two older widowed persons to marry late in life. The new spouse is often not so much a substitute for the deceased spouse as he is a buffer against the loneliness of old age.

Because of the five-year differential in life expectancy between males and females and because the custom in our society is for men to marry younger women, widows are much more plentiful than widowers. In 1960 there were more than 4.5 million widows aged 65 or over, compared to about 1.3 million widowers in the same age category.[26] Older women, therefore, are much more likely to be faced with the problem of adjusting to the loss of the spouse than are older men.

Organized religion and social organizations, such as senior citizens' clubs, perform an important function in helping women adjust to their status as widows. Unfortunately, these organizations have not been as successful in reaching widowers. One of the most pressing unsolved problems of old age is the problem of overcoming loneliness and social isolation.

[26] *Statistical Abstract, op. cit.,* table 27, p. 34.

Chapter 9. The aging and society

THROUGHOUT the preceding chapters we have examined some of the specific problems facing the aging and the implications of these problems for society in general. This chapter looks at aging from a broader perspective and examines the consequences of the increasing proportion of aged persons for society. The fact that in our population there is a continuous increase in the proportion of the 65-and-over age category could lead to profound changes in the structure of our society and the direction in which it is going.

The proportion of people aged 65 and over in the United States increased from 4.1 per cent in 1900 to more than 9 per cent in 1960; it has continued to increase since then.[1] Any category of citizens constituting as substantial a segment of the population as our older people possesses the potential to exert considerable influence on the present and future directions of American society.

In 1961, there were 18 states in which 10 per cent or more of the population was in the 65-and-over age category. Iowa led the nation with the largest proportion of older people, 12.0 per cent, followed by Missouri with 11.8 per cent. The largest concentrations of older people were found mostly in midwestern or New England states. There were 7 such midwestern states (Iowa, Missouri, Nebraska, Kansas, Minnesota, South Dakota, and Wisconsin) and 5 New England states (Vermont, Massachusetts, New Hampshire, Maine, and Rhode Island) among the 18. The other states were New York, Pennsylvania, Arkansas, Oklahoma, Oregon, and Florida.[2]

With the exception of Florida, these 18 states were characterized by a net loss of population through migration (or very slight gain), a large rural population, or a highly settled population. The old people in these states tend to be immobile. Most of them were born in their state of residence and have lived there all their lives. They frequently have been left behind by the out-migration of younger people.

[1] Arnold M. Rose, "The Subculture of the Aging: A Framework for Research in Social Gerontology," in Arnold M. Rose and Warren A. Peterson, eds., *Older People and Their Social World* (Philadelphia: F. A. Davis Company, Inc., 1965), p. 4.
[2] President's Council on Aging, *The Older American* (Washington, D.C.: U.S. Government Printing Office, 1963), table 2, pp. 62–63.

Florida is the exception, in that the large proportion of older people in Florida is due to in-migration from other states. Those older people who do migrate tend to move to Florida, California, Arizona, or Texas in search of warm, sunny climates. Because of the volume of migration into California and Arizona by people of all ages, however, these states do not have unusually high proportions of older people.[3]

Those states with the smallest proportions of older people tend to be those which might be characterized as the newer, frontier states. In 1961, Alaska, Hawaii, Nevada, New Mexico, Arizona, and Utah all had proportions of people 65 and over well below the national average. The only other two states in the Union which had less than 7 per cent of their populations in the 65-and-over age category were North and South Carolina. These are two atypical states; neither new nor frontier states. Alaska, with 2.4 per cent, had the smallest proportion of aged persons of any state in the Union.[4]

There are a few cities in the United States whose aged residents constitute a substantial proportion of the total population. The most extreme in this respect is St. Petersburg, Florida, where about one of every four inhabitants is 65 or older. Other cities with high proportions of older people are Pasadena, California; Long Beach, California; Portland, Oregon; Spokane, Washington; and Tacoma, Washington.[5]

It stands to reason that the larger the proportion of old people in a state or city, the more impact they will have upon the economic, political, and social fortunes of the area. It is not possible for a state or city to ignore the needs and wants of a substantial portion of its population.

Economic influences

The influence older people exert on the economy must be understood within the context of their economic position. The 1960 annual income figures for unattached persons aged 65 and over were: about 53 per cent, less than $1,000; about 24 per cent, between $1,000 and $2,000; and 10 per cent, $3,000 or more. Of the families in 1960 with heads of family in the 65-and-over age category, 50 per cent had annual incomes of less than

[3] *Ibid.*
[4] *Ibid.*
[5] T. Lynn Smith, "A Comparative Study of the Age Distribution of the Population of Major Cities in the United States," *Social Forces* XXXVIII (1960), reprinted in Clyde B. Vedder, ed., *Gerontology: A Book of Readings* (Springfield, Ill.: Charles C. Thomas, 1963), p. 186.

$2,900 and 25 per cent, of less than $1,600.[6] The incomes of the over-whelming majority of older people were very limited. Only a small minority had substantial incomes.

In addition to having low incomes, older people tend to have limited assets such as savings. In 1960, 20 per cent of those families headed by persons aged 65 or over had less than $1,000 in assets. About 40 per cent of the aged with incomes of less than $2,000 had very limited assets.[7]

However, families with older heads were less likely to have debts than families with younger heads. For one thing, older families were reluctant to purchase on credit. This reluctance was attributable to a distaste for credit buying rather than an inability to qualify for credit.

According to the 1960 Survey of Consumer Finances conducted by the Survey Research Center of the University of Michigan, 63 per cent of the families with heads 65 years or older owned their own homes, and 53 per cent owned their own homes mortgage free.[8]

In summary, in 1960 the typical family headed by a person of 65 years or over had a very limited and fixed income, limited assets, few debts, and—more often than not—a mortgage-free home. It should be noted, however, that the older family was likely to be a two-person family; therefore, its limited income and assets provided for fewer persons than was the case for younger families.

In spite of the limited incomes and assets of our older citizens, collectively they represent in excess of 37 billion dollars a year in purchasing power. Obviously, they constitute a very attractive consumer market. Realization of the potentialities of this market has led to the publication of such articles as "Expanding Markets: The Oldsters," which appeared in *The Nation's Business* in November 1957. This article described the aged population of the United States and analyzed its consumption patterns for the benefit of enterprising businessmen.

Since the consumption patterns of older people generally vary from those of younger people, the increasing demands for goods and services by older people are having substantial impact upon business and industry. Let us see how the consumption patterns of old people differ from those of the remainder of the population.

The pattern of expenditures of the small percentage of older families with substantial incomes differs only slightly from the pattern of expendi-

---

[6] Herbert E. Striner, "The Capacity of the Economy to Support Older People," in Harold L. Orbach and Clark Tibbitts, eds., *Aging and the Economy* (Ann Arbor: The University of Michigan Press, 1963), p. 18.

[7] Charles A. Lininger, "Some Aspects of the Economic Situation of the Aged: Recent Survey Findings," in Orbach and Tibbitts, *op. cit.*, pp. 75 and 78.

[8] *Ibid.*, p. 72.

tures for younger families. The oldsters may travel, for example, instead of going skiing. However, the older families with limited incomes do vary significantly from the remainder of the population in their pattern of expenditures.

In 1960–61 the Bureau of Labor Statistics of the U.S. Department of Labor conducted a survey of consumer expenditures for the urban United States.[9] By means of the findings of the survey, let us compare the expenditure patterns of older families with those of younger families. Two categories of older families were surveyed: those in which the head of the family was between the ages of 65 and 74, and those in which the head was 75 or over. For purposes of comparison, we will note the differences between the expenditure patterns for these two categories of older families and families in which the head was between the ages of 45 and 54. This particular age category was selected for comparison because it marks the time in life when the family is likely to be well established, when income is at its peak, and when the family is likely to be a two-person family, the children having left home.

For families in all age categories, the highest percentage of average total expenditures was for food; in the 45–54 category, it was 24 per cent. Older families spent proportionately more for food: in the 65–74 category it was 25.7 per cent and in the 75-and-over category, 26.7 per cent.

The second largest expenditure for families in all age categories was housing, including fuel, light, and refrigeration. Here again, the expenditure was proportionately higher for older families than for younger ones. Families in the 45–54 age category spent 17 per cent of their total expenditures on housing, compared to 21.9 per cent for those in the 65–74 category and 25.2 per cent for families in the 75-and-over category.

Household operation also consumed a greater percentage of the total expenditures of the older families than it did for the younger families. The percentage expenditure for families in the 45–54 category was 5.5, compared to 6.7 per cent for the families in the 65–74 category and 7.6 per cent for the families in 75-and-over category.

Older families had increasingly higher percentage expenditures for medical care. Families in the 45–54 age category spent 6 per cent of their total expenditures on medical care, those in the 65–74 category 9.4 per cent, and families in the 75-and-over category 12 per cent.

The only other consumption category in which the proportionate expenditure was higher for the older families was the purchase of reading material. The percentage expenditure for families in the 45–54 category

---

[9] *Consumer Expenditures and Income, Urban United States, 1960–61.* The Bureau, Washington, D.C., 1964, BLS Report No. 237–38.

was 0.9, compared to 1.1 per cent for the families in the 65–74 category and 1.2 per cent for the families in the 75-and-over category.

There were no significant differences in proportionate expenditures for personal care by families in the different age categories. Families in all age categories spent between 2.7 and 2.9 per cent of their total expenditures on personal care items such as haircuts, permanents, cosmetics, and so on.

In all other expenditure categories surveyed, the proportionate expenditures were greater for the younger families than they were for the two categories of older families. Younger families spent proportionately more for the purchase of home furnishings, clothing, transportation, recreation, education, tobacco, and alcoholic beverages.

Sidney Goldstein suggests two major reasons for the relationship between family-age level and pattern of expenditures:

First, the different stages of the life cycle have associated with them quite different needs for goods and services, and these different needs are reflected in the patterns of differential expenditures among the various age segments. Second, because the average amount of money available for meeting consumer needs varies significantly as the family unit passes through the various stages of the life cycle, the way in which this money is allocated must be changed so as first to insure the satisfaction of the more essential needs and only secondarily to meet those needs on which more money would ordinarily be spent if it were available.[10]

It should be remembered that, although older families generally spend a larger proportion of their total expenditures on food and housing than do younger families, it does not follow that they spend more money. The more limited incomes of the older families provide them with less money to spend on food and housing than is the case with younger families. The fact that the older family can afford fewer luxury items than the younger families also results in proportionately larger expenditures on such necessities as food and housing.

The proportionately larger expenditure for household operation by older families reflects the greater amount of time they spend at home and, conceivably, their need to purchase services younger householders can perform for themselves. The greater amount of time spent at home is also reflected by their proportionately greater expenditures on reading materials and their proportionately smaller expenditures on recreational activities outside the home. Here, also, lies a partial explanation for the lesser expenditure on transportation by members of older families. They don't go

[10] "Changing Income and Consumption Patterns of the Aged, 1950–1960," *Journal of Gerontology*, XX (1965), p. 461.

out as often as younger people and they may not own automobiles. When they do go out, they are likely to use public transportation.

Younger people, being more sensitive to current fashions and having more money available, spend proportionately more on home furnishings and clothing. Because of their limited incomes and life expectancies, older people are frequently reluctant to purchase new furniture; they make do with what they have. Generally they feel the same way about the purchase of clothing. Staying at home much of the time, they feel no need to dress up; and furthermore, they feel that there are better ways to spend their money than on clothes.

Advancing age is generally accompanied by declining health; therefore, it is understandable that the proportionate expenditure for medical care is higher for older families than it is for the younger families. In the case of medical care, the amount of money spent as well as the proportion of expenditures increases with increasing age. Older people generally have more frequent and larger medical bills than younger people.

Educational expenditures are proportionately less in older families because the older families have fewer dependent children and the oldsters, themselves, consider education a luxury item rather than a necessity.

There is a very logical explanation for the decreasing expenditures for tobacco and alcoholic beverages among older people. With women living about five years longer than men, older people are predominantly females. In 1960 among those aged 65 and over, there were approximately 828 men for every 1,000 women in the United States.[11] But women smoke less and consume less alcohol than men and, as the men die off, total expenditures for tobacco and alcoholic beverages by the elderly decrease.

The steadily increasing older population represents a constantly expanding consumer market which will come to have more and more influence upon the quantities and kinds of goods and services produced. Imaginative business people are turning their attention to the development of new products that will meet the demands of the elderly. One obvious example here is the boom in specialized housing facilities for the aged.[12] Another example is the development of the electric buggy designed to meet the neighborhood transportation needs of the elderly. As older people make their demands known to business and industry, dramatic changes in business and industrial activities are likely to occur.

The labor market is also subject to economic pressure from the older population. The government and organized labor have become increasingly concerned about the prospects for full employment. Automation and

[11] U.S. Bureau of the Census, *Statistical Abstract of the United States: 1961* (82d ed.; Washington, D.C., 1961), table 19, p. 28.
[12] See Chapter 4.

increased productive efficiency will have continuing effects on the man-
power needs of the nation. The problem is one of making the available
jobs go round. Earlier retirement would help relieve some of the pressure
on the labor market; but the increasing life expectancy is already adding to
the length of the retirement period. If older workers are to be removed
earlier from the labor force to make room for younger workers, then more
substantial provisions will need to be made for their economic well-being
in retirement. A special panel commissioned by President Lyndon B.
Johnson to study the economic future of the United States came up with
the recommendation that a guaranteed annual income be made available
to every family, whether or not members of the family work. Though there
may be merit to such a proposal, particularly in the case of older families, it
is not likely to be implemented in the near future.

Political influences

Politicians have become increasingly aware of the potential political
power that resides in our older population. In each succeeding campaign
the vote of the older citizen is wooed with ever increasing fervor. Political
strategists cringed when Barry Goldwater made critical remarks about the
Social Security program during the presidential campaign of 1964. The
vote of the older citizen was equated in importance with the Negro vote as
a factor that could swing the election either way. Is the politician's concern
with the aged voter warranted? How potent a political force is our older
population?

Certain issues are of vital importance to aging Americans. Obviously, the
Social Security program, pension plans, medical plans, low-cost housing,
and taxes have high interest value. As a matter of fact, most of the political
issues that concern the aged are economic: security and adequate financial
resources are among the major sources of worry. Politicians attuned to the
concerns of their constituents tailor their platforms accordingly. In those
areas having large numbers of older registered voters, proposals that will
benefit the elderly are likely to be conspicuously included among campaign
promises. School bonds have rough sledding in districts with aging populations.

Older people are not unique among our voting publics. Like most voters,
they support those proposals that benefit them directly, oppose those that
will cost them money, and ignore those considered neither a direct threat
nor a direct benefit. The older voter will vote for an increase in old age
pensions and, at the same time, against a rise in taxes designed to finance

the increased benefits. At first glance, this behavior may seem inconsistent, but viewed from the perspective of the older person it is not. He has a very modest, fixed income. Every dollar he gets is vitally important to him. He will fight for every additional dollar he can get and protest every increase in taxes that will drain off his funds. The occasional irresponsible proposals made to abolish taxes often meet with substantial support from the older population in spite of the fact that their incomes are largely supported by taxes.

Many older people do not look upon school bonds and school taxes as an investment in the future of their country. Rather, they look upon them as an immediate threat to their incomes. Old people may vote against school bonds or taxes even though their own grandchildren are directly involved.

According to popular belief, the young are liberal in their political views and sympathetic to social change; the old are conservative and defenders of the status quo. Numerous studies lend support to the proposition that conservative tendencies increase with age. Of course, there are exceptions to the rule. There are many young people who are conservative (not all John Birch Society members are old ladies in tennis shoes) and many old people who are liberal. But generally, old people tend to be more conservative than young people. A philosophical metamorphosis is not the explanation for the drift to conservatism. Most people are not philosophical about their politics. The explanation lies, rather, in what the politicians call "gut politics." People take political positions in keeping with their life situations. Young people frequently have little at stake. They can afford to be liberal and sympathetic to change, because they have little to lose if change takes place. Older people distrust liberalism and change because they hold dear the things they have. They have the investment of a lifetime at stake.

However, even the most conservative people support change in areas of benefit to them. In a study of older people, Angus Campbell found that they supported government programs for full employment and low-cost medical care, but did not support government programs to assure equal rights to Negroes or to build more schools.[13] Conservatism, then, is a function of the social situation in which the person finds himself. People tend to be conservative in some situations and liberal in others. Because the situations in which the older person finds himself are most amenable to what is commonly thought of as a conservative position, the older person is seen as being conservative.

We have now established that there are issues in which old people are vitally interested. Being interested, however, is not sufficient to make older

---

[13] "Social and Psychological Determinants of Voting Behavior," in Wilma Donahue and Clark Tibbitts, eds., *Politics of Age* (Ann Arbor: The University of Michigan Press, 1962), pp. 94–95.

people a significant political force. They must also be politically active. According to Campbell, political involvement increases with age. Older people are more interested in politics, they follow politics in the mass media more, and they participate more actively than younger people. While only about 50 per cent of the people in their early twenties vote in presidential elections, slightly more than 80 per cent of those in their sixties and about 75 per cent of those in their seventies vote. About two-thirds of those over 80 are still able and interested enough to vote.[14]

Contrary to popular belief, elderly people are not overwhelmingly Republicans. Persons over 65 are split about equally between the two parties. In all younger age categories there are more Democrats than Republicans.[15] Rather than switching parties as they grow older, people are more likely to become firmly entrenched in the party of their choice. Older people identify more strongly with one or the other of the major parties than do younger people.

Whether our older citizens will ever constitute a monolithic voting block is questionable. Some factors would seem to support such a development; other factors, however, would seem to make such a development unlikely. Let us examine the relevant factors, pro and con. Arguments in favor of the development of a voting block of older people include:

1. The existence of salient issues. Pension plans have always had wide support from our older citizens. The Townsend Movement of the 1930's developed a lot of political steam. Townsend Clubs sprang up all over the country in response to Dr. Francis E. Townsend's proposal that the government give each person over the age of 60 a monthly pension of $200. The movement's followers came closest to becoming a voting block in 1936, when Dr. Townsend threw his support behind William Lemke's unsuccessful Union Party. In 1958, George McLain, then champion of California's senior citizens, had solid support from the elderly in his unsuccessful try at the Democratic nomination for governor. McLain ran on a platform that included a comprehensive program of benefits for the elderly.

2. The high degree of interest older people have in politics and their high participation rate in political activities. Since such a high percentage of older people vote, they are in a position to exercise political influence out of proportion to their numbers. Also, since they are more politically active than younger people, they have the potential for waging campaigns that will effectively woo other voters to their cause.

There are equally convincing reasons, however, for a voting block not to develop among older people. These reasons include the following:

1. The aged do not constitute a primary reference group for older

[14] *Ibid.*, pp. 90–91.
[15] *Ibid.*, p. 92.

people. That is, old people generally do not see themselves primarily as being members of a group composed of the elderly. They identify themselves more readily with other groups of which they are members. For instance, they identify themselves with their occupations, their families, their political parties, their churches, or their social groups. The wealthy elderly person votes as a wealthy person rather than as an elderly person. The elderly Democrat votes as a Democrat rather than an elderly person.

It is frequently painful to take the aged as one's reference group, because being aged in our society has low prestige. People look upon old age as the most distasteful stage of the life cycle. They only identify themselves with the aged when some particularly salient issue, such as pensions, is at stake.

2. The aged are evenly split between the major political parties, and they are highly partisan members of their parties. Socioeconomic status is a more important factor than age in determining party affiliation. The low-income and blue-collar people usually identify themselves with the Democratic party; the affluent and white-collar people usually identify with the Republican party. Furthermore, older people perceive greater divergence in the philosophies of the two parties than do younger people, because they remember the parties as they were in earlier days. The clear-cut schism among the elderly in their political allegiances operates against the development of a monolithic political stance by older people.

3. Where there are local concentrations of older people, there is a higher probability that they will behave as a block. In some local elections, older people have been known to vote as a block and influence the outcome. It is obvious that in a community like St. Petersburg, Florida, the older population will be a potent political force to be reckoned with. On the national level, however, older people are widely dispersed throughout the population. Their geographic and social dispersion works against the development of a voting block. Voting blocks develop most readily where communication is frequent and effective.

4. Issues that become particularly salient tend to be absorbed into the platforms of the major political parties. This inhibits the development of blocks made up exclusively of old people, because the goals of the old people can be pursued within the existing machinery of the major parties. When the Townsend Movement threatened to become a major political force in the thirties, the Democratic party came out with the Social Security program, and enacted it in 1935. This stole much of the thunder from the Townsend Movement as a separate political force, and its importance gradually receded.

Historically, special-interest groups have been singularly unsuccessful in the United States in their attempts to start new political parties. The two major parties characteristically absorb into their own programs the sounder ideas of the special-interest groups. For this reason, it is unlikely that we will ever see a major political party that is uniquely an "old people's party." The needs and demands of our older citizens will be met within the frameworks of our two existing major parties. Within these parties, however, our older citizens will have an increasingly important voice.

Social influences

Society consists of a complex network of social organizations in a continuous process of change. There is a continuous turnover in the members of the various social organizations as well as a turnover in the organizations themselves. The characteristics of the members of such a social group affect the organizational milieu and the manner in which the organization operates. An organization changes as its membership changes. At any one point in time, some organizations are coming into being and others are going out of existence. Society, then, is as much process as it is structure.

There are two basic ways in which older people affect society: (1) they change society by introducing new social organizations into the social system, and (2) they change the existing social organizations through their participation in them. A number of local, state, and national organizations that have come into being are specifically older people's organizations. On the national level are the American Association of Retired Persons, The National Retired Teachers Association, The National Association of Retired Civil Employees, and the Senior Citizens of America. On the state level are such organizations as the California League of Senior Citizens. On the local level are innumerable organizations that are known by such names as Senior Citizen Clubs, Golden Agers Clubs, Keen-Agers Clubs, and so on.

These organizations are designed to meet the social, recreational, educational, welfare, and political needs of the elderly. For example, the affiliated American Association of Retired Persons and The National Retired Teachers Association, with a combined membership of more than 800,000, have four major goals: (1) education of the members, with emphasis upon enriching the later years of life; (2) informational services to individuals, including advice on creative activities and interests, suggestions on how to maintain income, and suggestions as to where to go for help with personal problems; (3) establishing programs of affiliated groups on the local level; and (4) nonprofit services, including low-cost hospitalization, discount drugs, and a tour service.[16] Obviously, the expansion and proliferation of such organizations for the elderly have an impact upon society.

Existing organizations with large numbers of elderly members are influenced by the older members' interests, attitudes, and values. Companies in which the management and employees are elderly are likely to differ considerably from companies with young personnel. Whereas the established, conservative companies with long histories behind them often have older personnel, the new, dynamic companies in the newer industries tend to have younger personnel.

Legislatures with large numbers of older lawmakers tend to perform differently than those in which the lawmakers are younger. Even in those cases where the older lawmakers are not numerous, they are often able to exert considerable influence upon the legislative process because of their greater seniority. Action by the Congress of the United States has often been restrained by crusty old congressmen firmly entrenched as the chairmen of key committees.

Does the prospect of increasing numbers of older persons in our society portend a gerontocracy in our future? We have come to the realization that our older citizens do constitute a social force. This fact is demonstrated by the passage of the Older Americans Act of 1965, the Medicare Act of 1965, and the founding of the Administration on Aging within the Department of Health, Education, and Welfare. However, the proportion of older people in the United States is not likely to increase greatly beyond its present level unless there are some startling breakthroughs in medical science. Furthermore, the kind of group consciousness necessary to make possible concerted activities by the elderly is unlikely to develop.[17] Our older persons will continue to play an important role in the future of the United States, but it will not be a controlling role.

[16] Ethel Percy Andrus, "Older People Observe Their Organizational Roles: Social Influence Organizations," in Donahue and Tibbitts, *op. cit.*, pp. 156–157.

[17] For a dissenting opinion, see Arnold M. Rose, "Group Consciousness among the Aging," in Rose and Peterson, *op. cit.*, pp. 19–36.

Index